Orthodox Wisdom

FaR

To Aidan Hart

Published in 2023 by FeedARead.com Publishing. Financed by **The Arts Council of Great Britain**
Copyright ©FatherSpyridonBailey

Contents

Introduction

We proclaim the Church to be One, Holy, Catholic and Apostolic. It is One because it is the united Body of Christ proclaiming a single faith and sharing in a life of prayer and in the Holy Mysteries. The Church is Holy because it is the Body of Christ, and because the Holy Spirit is alive in us and is helping us to repent of those things which prevent us from being holy. It is Catholic because it is universal; it is created by God that all men may find salvation within its boundaries, and all men are created to exist within it (though many reject this holy calling). It is Apostolic, because the life, faith and authority given to the Apostles continue in its members today. We do not believe that the Church is Apostolic solely because it was the Apostles who first received the Holy spirit at Pentecost, or that our bishops continue to exercise the Apostles' authority and gifts through the centuries, it is more than this. The Orthodox Church is Apostolic because the Apostles are living members of our Church, they continue to pray for us, and the same Christ Who revealed Himself to them reveals Himself to us in our time.

The saints of all ages have acquired what we long for. They have endured the hardships of this world as we endure; they have struggled against their passions as we are now called to struggle, and they have wept in repentance and cried out to God in prayer. In the face of human weakness, they have been victorious, they have been granted entry into God's Kingdom, they have demonstrated to us that we must not lose hope or imagine that the spiritual road is too much for us. And in their victory, they have shared their wisdom to guide others.

This collection comes from that wisdom. Here are words to comfort, warn, encourage and sustain us. Here are words to warm our hearts for God, to remind us of our human dignity and the spiritual work we must accept if we are to draw closer to Christ. Most of the guidance found here comes from those recognized as saints, and some from those yet to be formally canonized.

When we sing the hymns of the Church, we use words inspired by God from people who have entered deeply into their souls. The words speak from a place of self-knowledge that few of us will enter. But when we use these words, our own souls respond from a place more profound than any conscious thoughts of the mind. So it is with many teachings from the saints: they express truth and reality which few of us are able to find but which can touch us deeply.

The intention here is not use their words to make arguments or prove points: it is just as foolish to select quotations from the fathers for this purpose as it is for those who do so from the Holy Scriptures.

In 1988 I met a monk from Mount Athos who revealed to me something of the reality of God's Church. One piece of advice he gave was that when

inspired by something I read, I should write it down so
that I would always have a source of inspiration to
turn to. After thirty-five years of following his advice
this book is a selection of those sources of inspiration
They are offered here in the hope that other hearts
will be inspired by them.

Priest Spyridon 2023

God's Love

Sinners that repent are still saved; both publicans and fornicators cleansed by repentance enter into the Kingdom of Heaven.

The compassionate God still calls to Himself all that have turned away, and He awaits them and promises them mercy.

The loving Father still receives His prodigal sons come back from a far country and He opens the doors of His house and clothes them in the best robe, and gives them each a ring on their hand and shoes on their feet and commands all the saints to rejoice in them.

St. Tikhon of Zadonsk

A certain monk told me that when he was very sick, his mother said to his father, "How our little boy is suffering. I would gladly give myself to be cut up into pieces if that would ease his suffering." Such is the love of God for people. He pitied people so much that he wanted to suffer for them, like their own mother, and even more. But no one can understand this great love without the grace of the Holy Spirit.

St. Silouan the Athonite

The human mind is given the rational power of God – we have the mind of Christ (Cor. 2, 16), says the Holy apostle Paul. To the human heart, the heart of Christ is given. The perishable is made immortal. Those naked and wounded by sin and by passions are adorned in Divine glory. Those who hunger and thirst are sated and assuaged by the nourishing and soul-strengthening Word of God and by the most pure Body and Divine Blood of Christ. The inconsolable are consoled. Those ravaged by the devil have been – and continue to be – delivered.
St. John of Kronstadt

If we become aware of how God cares for us like an all-loving Father, and even more gently, like an adoring mother, then our hearts will be filled to overflowing with ardent and reverent love for Him.
Archbishop Averky (Taushev)

God loves us very much; He has us in mind in each and every moment and He protects us. We should know this and not be afraid of anything.
St. Porphyrios

Sinners that repent are still saved; both publicans and fornicators cleansed by repentance enter into the Kingdom of Heaven.
The compassionate God still calls to Himself all that have turned away, and He awaits them and promises them mercy.

The loving Father still receives His prodigal sons come back from a far country and He opens the doors of His house and clothes them in the best robe, and gives them each a ring on their hand and shoes on their feet and commands all the saints to rejoice in them.
St. Tikhon of Zadonsk

Human nature is deified for the sake of the boundless compassion of the Son of God; and its sins are purified; the defiled are sanctified. The ailing are healed. Upon those in dishonour are boundless honour and glory bestowed. Those in darkness are enlightened by the Divine light of grace and reason.
St. John of Kronstadt

Love does not reflect. Love is simple. Love never mistakes. Likewise believe and trust without reflection, for faith and trust are also simple; or better: God, in whom we believe and in whom we trust, is an incomplex Being, as He is also simply love.
St. John of Kronstadt

The devil will represent the Lord's fact to you as terrible and unmerciful, rejecting your prayer and repentance; but remember the Saviour's own words, full of every hope and boldness for us: `Him that cometh to Me, I will in no wise cast out'; and `Come unto Me, all ye that labour and are heavy laden' – with sins and iniquities, and wiles and calumnies of

the devil – and I will give you rest.'
St. John of Kronstadt

The Lord calls to him all sinners; He opens His arms wide, even to the worst among them. Gladly He takes them in His arms, if only they will come to Him.
St. Macarius of Optina

God loves us more than a father, mother, friend, or any else could love, and even more than we are able to love ourselves.
St. John Chrysostom

Even if we have thousands of acts of great virtue to our credit, our confidence in being heard must be based on God's mercy and His love for men. Even if we stand at the very summit of virtue, it is by mercy that we shall be saved.
St. John Chrysostom

If we call upon the saints with faith and love, then they will immediately hear us. The faith is the connecting element on our part, and love on theirs, as well as ours; for they are in God, and we are in God Who is Love.
St. John of Kronstadt

If we do commit some sin again, we should without delay ask forgiveness once again, and the Lord will forgive us, for He came not to save the righteous but

the sinners, i.e. those who acknowledge their sins.
Abbot Nikon Vorobiev

Have confidence in the compassion of our Creator. Reflect well on what you are now doing, and keep before you the things you have done. Lift up your eyes to the overflowing compassion of heaven, and while He waits for you, draw near in tears to our merciful Judge. Having before your mind that He is a Just Judge, do not take your sins lightly; and having also in mind that He is compassionate, do not despair. The God-Man gives man confidence before God.
St. Gregory the Great

The cross is the gate of mysteries.
St. Isaac the Syrian

As a handful of sand thrown into the ocean, so are the sins of all flesh as compared with the mind of God.
St. Isaac the Syrian

Thirst after Jesus, and He will satisfy you with His love.
St. Isaac the Syrian

If the soul be afflicted it will receive mercy from God.
Abba Poemen

God saith unto thee, "If thou wishest Me to have

mercy on thee, thou must have mercy on thy brother and then I will have mercy on thee; and if thou wishest Me to forgive thee, thou also must forgive thy brother, and then I will forgive thee." Can any blame rest on God? God forbid. But the cause resteth with us, and if we wish we are able to live.
Abba Poemen

It was the ground that God cursed, not Adam. And He cursed the serpent and the fire was prepared originally for the devil and his legions not for mankind.
St. Irenaeus

There is more mercy in God than there are sins in us, confess your sins at once whatever they may be.
St. Tikhon of Zadensk

Our Lord visibly carried Peter on the sea to teach us that He was also invisibly carrying him on dry land.
St. Ephraim the Syrian

An old man was asked by one who toiled, "Is the repentance of sinners accepted by God?"
"Tell me, if thy cloak were to be torn in rags, wouldst thou throw it away?"
And he said unto him, "No, I would mend it and use it again."
And the old man said unto him, "If thou wouldst show pity upon thy garment which hath no feeling, shall

not God show pity on that which He hath fashioned, and which is His work?"
Sayings of the Desert Fathers

The all-good Providence of God always arranges what is most beneficial for us, while in our ignorance, we very often strive for the very opposite.
St. Ambrose of Optina

You should continually and unceasingly call to mind all the blessings which God in His love has bestowed on you in the past, and still bestows for the salvation of your soul. You must not let forgetfulness of evil or laziness make you grow unmindful of these many and great blessings, and so pass the rest of your life uselessly and ungratefully.
St. Mark the Ascetic

It is God, Who is merciful and grants everyone what he needs, Who is building him up when He gives him more than he needs; in doing so He shows the abundance of His love for men and teaches him to give thanks. When He does not grant him what he needs, He makes him compensate for the thing he needs through the working of the mind and teaches him patience.
St. Dorotheos of Gaza

Asceticism

Drive away with the hand of humility every transitory joy, as being unworthy of it, but by readily admitting it, you receive a wolf instead of a shepherd.
St. John Climacus

The flesh is an ungrateful and treacherous friend. The more you care for it, the more it injures you.
St. John Climacus

From gluttony arises every kind of carnal impurity.
St. Gregory Palamas

While fasting, let us purify our hearts, sanctify our souls, and trample down all vices.
St. Theodore Studite

Devils take great delight in fullness, and drunkenness and bodily comfort. Fasting possesses great power and it works glorious things. To fast is to banquet with angels.
St. Athanasius the Great

This world troubleth thee because its care is in thy mind, and the love of it is in thy body, and its

pleasures are in thy heart; forsake the world and it will depart from thee.
Sayings of the Desert Fathers.

It is more difficult to make a genuine Christian than it is a cathedral.
Elder Cleopa of Romania

No one who looks for comfort can expect to attain interior peace.
Elder Michael of Valaam

Nobody can become a Christian by being lazy. It needs work, lots of work.
St. Porphyrios

For anything that is quickly obtained is also easily lost, whereas everything found with toil is also kept with careful watching.
St. Isaac the Syrian

O glutton, bent on the worship of your own belly! It is better for you to cast a live coal into your stomach than the fried foods of rulers and princes.
St. Isaac the Syrian

Whoever does not voluntarily withdraw himself from the causes of the passions is involuntarily drawn away by sin. These are the causes of sin: wine,

women, riches, and robust health of body. Not that by their nature these things are sins, but that nature readily inclines towards the sinful passions on their account, and for this reason man must guard himself against them with great care.
St. Isaac the Syrian

Of course, it would be easier to get to paradise with a full stomach, all snuggled up in a soft feather-bed, but what is required is to carry one's cross along the way, for the kingdom of God is not attained by enduring one or two troubles, but many!
St. Anthony of Optina

Self-opposition and self-forcing, these are the true aspects of zeal born in the soul, forming the beginning of asceticism. Both of these comprise the struggle of man with himself (podvig).
St. Theophan the Recluse

As a moth gnaws a garment, so doth envy consume a man.
St. John Chrysostom

It is folly to abstain all day long from food, but fail to abstain from sin and selfishness.
St. John Chrysostom

Turning away from all wickedness means keeping our tongue in check, restraining our anger, avoiding all

gossip, lying and swearing. To abstain from these things, herein lies the true fast.
St. John Chrysostom

Accept the fast as an experienced educator by whom the Church teaches us piety.
St. John Chrysostom

If, therefore, we desire to be set free and to enjoy perfect freedom, let us learn to cut off our desires.
St. Dorotheos of Gaza

Satiety is extremely harmful for the soul. Whoever overindulges in food or drink is incapable of spiritual exercises and can neither pray nor reflect on anything divine, because excess in food draws a person into laziness, sleepiness, idleness, idle talk, ludicrous behavior, and a great multitude of impure thoughts and desires.
Metropolitan Gregory (Postnikov) of St. Petersburg

Because we put ourselves out of the sight of God we are led captive by the passions of the body.
Abba Theona

To yield and give way to our passions is the lowest slavery, even as to rule over them is the only liberty.
St. Justin Martyr

Excessive conveniences make life difficult for people.
Saint Paisios of Mount Athos

Our religion is perfectly and profoundly conceived.
What is simple is also what is most precious.
Accordingly, in your spiritual life engage in your daily
contest simply, easily, and without force. The soul is
sanctified and purified through the study of the
Fathers, through the memorization of the psalms and
of portions of Scripture, through the signing of hymns
and through the repetition of the Jesus Prayer.
Devote your efforts, therefore, to these spiritual
things and ignore all the other things.
St. Porphyrios

One should not think about the doings of God when
one's stomach is full; on a full stomach there can be
no vision of the Divine mysteries.
St. Seraphim of Sarov

Do not have Jesus Christ on your lips and the world in
your heart.
St. Ignatius of Antioch

The zealot who labours, forces himself, opposes
himself.
St. Theophan the Recluse

Why do demons wish to excite in us gluttony,
fornication, greed, anger, rancour and other passions

So that the mind, under their weight, should be unable to pray as it ought; for when the passions of our irrational part begin to act, they prevent the mind from acting rationally.
St. Nilus of Sinai

Let us be satisfied simply with what sustains our present life, not what pampers it.
St. Maximos the Confessor

A small but persistent discipline is a great force; for a soft drop persistently hollows out even a rock.
St. Isaac the Syrian

Happiness can only be achieved by looking inward and learning to enjoy whatever life has and this requires transforming greed into gratitude.
St. John Chrysostom

Let him who has comfort in this world not hope to receive eternal comfort. For the Kingdom of Heaven is not made up of those who are comforted here, but of those who are persecuted in this life in much affliction and distress.
St. Athanasios

The chief evil with relation to the body is love for the body and pitying it. This takes away all the soul's authority over the body and makes the soul the slave of the body. And on the contrary, one who does not

spare the body will not be disturbed in whatever he does by apprehensions born of blind love of life. How fortunate is one who is trained to this from childhood!
St. Theophan the Recluse

Shun the satisfactions of this age, so as to be happy in the age to come. Do not be negligent, letting the days pass by 'till unexpectedly they come looking for you and you arrive at the straits of your anguish and the 'horror-faces' surround you and drag you off violently to their dark place of terror and anguish. Do not be sad when you are cursed by men; be sad and sigh when you sin — this is the true curse — and when you go away bearing the sores of your sins.
St. Pachomius the Great

You will not be able to cut down the passions attacking you unless you first leave untilled the soil from which they are fed.
Ilias the Presbyter

This is the sum of the mystery: to be corpses to the world but alive to God.
St. Theodore the Studite

Rouse yourselves! The world which you worship only flatters you. The heaviness of your flesh should not keep you back from our Saviour - the God of spirits and of all flesh. If you continue to drowse, you will imperceptibly fall under the influence of the evil spirits, who are anxious for the company even of swine. Be careful that you become not possessed by a devil.

St. Sebastian Dabovich

Penitential feelings are the sign of true asceticism, whoever runs away from them runs away from the true path.

St. Theophan the Recluse

Let us put God before our eyes continually; remember death and Christ our Redeemer; hate the world and everything which is therein; hate the world and all bodily pleasure; die unto this life, so that thou mayest live unto God, for God will require it of thee on the day of judgement. Be hungry and thirsty, and naked; weep and mourn; watch and groan in the heart; examine thyself to see if thou art worthy of God. Love labour and tribulation, so that thou mayest find God, and treat with contempt and despise the body, so that thy soul may live.

St. Anthony the Great

Everything that goes to excess comes from the demons.

Abba Poemen

He who is ignorant of the enemy's ambush is easily slain; and he who does not know the causes of the

passions is soon brought low.
St. Mark the Ascetic

When I work, I eat the fruit of my wages; but if I do
not work, I eat charity.
Abba Silvanus

To deny oneself means to give up one's bad habits; to
root out of the heart all that ties us to the world; not
to cherish bad thoughts or desires; to suppress every
evil thought; not to desire to do anything out of self
love, but to do everything out of love for God.
St. Innocent of Alaska

I can live on 100 grams of bread. This bread is blessed
by God because it is necessary, but not 110 grams.
That 10 grams is cursed because it is stolen and it
belongs to him who is hungry.
St. Kosmas Aitolos

No one whose stomach is full can fight mentally
against the demon of unchastity. Our initial struggle
therefore must be to gain control of our stomach and
to bring our body into subjection not only through
fasting but also through vigils, labors and spiritual
reading, and through concentrating our heart on fear
of Gehenna and on longing for the kingdom of heaven.
St. John Cassian

Through our anxiety about worldly things we hinder

the soul from enjoying divine blessings and we bestow on the flesh greater care and comfort than are good for it. We nourish it with what is harmful and thus make it an adversary, so that it not only wavers in battle but, because of over-indulgence, it fights vigorously against the soul, seeking honours and rewards.
Venerable Nilus the Faster of Sinai

One should nourish the soul with the word of God: for the word of God, as St. Gregory the Theologian says, is angelic bread, by which are nourished souls who hunger for God. Most of all, one should occupy oneself with reading the New Testament and the Psalter, which one should do standing up. From this there occurs enlightenment in the mind, which is in the mind, which is changed by a Divine change.
St. Seraphim of Sarov

Just as a basic concern is to be careful of anything that might be harmful to our physical health, so our spiritual concern should watch out for anything that might harm our spiritual life and the work of faith and salvation. Therefore, carefully and attentively assess your inner impulses: are they from God or from the spirit of evil?
St. John of Shangai

The person who does not despise all material things, glory and bodily comfort, even his own rights, cannot

cut off his own will, nor can he be delivered from wrath and sadness or comfort his neighbour.
Abba Dorotheos

If you want to serve God, prepare your heart not for food, not for drink, not for rest, not for ease, but for suffering, so that you may endure all temptations, trouble and sorrow. Prepare for severities, fasts, spiritual struggles and many afflictions, for "by many afflictions is it appointed to us to enter the Kingdom of Heaven" (Acts 14,22); 'The Heavenly Kingdom is taken by force, and the who use force seize it.' (Mat 11:12).
St. Sergius of Radonezh

When someone begins to say, 'What does it matter if say that word, eat that little morsel, feast my eyes on that?' He falls into bad habits and runs the risk of gradually falling into insensibility. For both virtues and vices start from slight things and lead to greater ones, either good or bad.
Archbishop Averky (Taushev)

A wandering mind is made stable by reading, vigil and prayer. Flaming lust is extinguished by hunger, labour and solitude. Stirrings of anger are calmed by psalmody, magnanimity and mercifulness. All this has its effect when used at its proper time and in due measure. Everything untimely or without proper measure is short-lived; and short-lived things are

more harmful than useful.
Abba Evagrius the Monk

We, who are slothful and weak-willed, remain hardened, and our fruits never ripen; for we have not the resolve to labour without sparing ourselves, in order to ripen in good works and rightly be gathered into the storehouse of life.
St. Ephraim the Syrian

Men of the world love the world because they have not yet discovered its bitterness. They are still blind in soul and do not see what is hiding behind this fleeting joy.
Elder Joseph the Hesychast

Steep and thorny is the path that leads to the Heavenly Kingdom. What is your path? It is the struggle unto blood against fleshly passions and self-love. Self-love is the soil upon which grow passions, emptiness of life, and sorrow.
Archbishop Seraphim (Sobolev) of Bogucharsk

The message of this universal temptation that attacks men today - quite openly in its secular forms, but usually more hidden in its religious forms - is: Live for the present, enjoy yourself, relax, be comfortable.
Father Seraphim Rose

Beware of passionate attachments to the world.

Although they deceive you with peace and comfort, they are so fleeting that you do not notice how you are deprived of them, and in their place come sorrow, longing, despondency, and no comfort whatsoever.
St. Leonid of Optina

All possible sins and passions are ready to break into the soul, and strive to do so at every moment.
But fight against them valiantly and vigilantly unto your last breath, looking upon them as dreams of your imagination, as illusions of the spirits of evil.
St. John of Kronstadt

It is necessary for a Christian to fast, in order to clear his mind, to rouse and develop his feelings, and to stimulate his will to useful activity. These three human capabilities we darken and stifle above all by 'surfeiting, and drunkenness, and cares of this life' (Lk. 21:34).
St. John of Kronstadt

There is nothing more dangerous than self-indulgence. It prepares the ground for all the vices because it chases out from the soul the fear of God.
St. Dorotheos of Gaza

Prayer

Prayer does not consist merely in standing and bowing your body or in reading written prayers....it is possible to pray at all times, in all places, with mind and spirit. You can lift up your mind and heart to God while walking, sitting, working, in a crowd and in solitude. His door is always open, unlike man's. We can always say to Him in our hearts Lord, Lord have mercy.
St. Tikhon of Zadonsk

Whatever you are doing, with whomever you are speaking, whether you are going somewhere or sitting, let your mind be with the Lord. You will forget yourself, and stray from this path; but again turn to the Lord and rebuke yourself with sorrow. This is the discipline of spiritual attentiveness.
St. Theophan the Recluse

Only the benumbed soul doesn't pray. Preserve in yourselves the feeling of need, and you will always have stimulation for prayer.
St. Theophan the Recluse

A sober man of prayer shoots arrows against them,

and they stay far away from him, not daring to approach, and fearing the defeat which they have already experienced.

If they succeed in something, it is due to our blundering. We slacken our attention, or allow ourselves to be distracted by their phantoms, and they immediately come and disturb us more boldly.

If you do not come to your senses in time they will whirl you about; but if a soul does come to its senses they again recoil and spy from afar to see whether it is possible to approach again somehow.

So be sober, watch, and pray—and the enemies will do nothing to you.

St. Theophan the Recluse

Fasting is universal temperance, prayer is universal communication with God; the former defends from the outside, whereas the latter from within directs a fiery weapon against the enemies. The demons can sense a faster and man of prayer from a distance, and they run far away from him so as to avoid a painful blow.

St. Theophan the Recluse

Prayer is the test of everything: if prayer is right everything is right.

St. Theophan the Recluse

Turn your mind towards Him continually. Learn to love prayer, familiar converse with the Lord. What

counts above all is love, passionate love for the Lord, for Christ the Bridegroom. Become worthy of Christ's love. In order not to live in darkness, turn on the switch of prayer so that divine light may flood your soul. Christ will appear in the depths of your being. There, in the deepest and most inward part, is the Kingdom of God. The Kingdom of God is within you [Luke 17:21].
St. Porphyrios

The Lord Himself will teach us how to pray. We won't learn prayer on our own, nor will anyone else teach us it. Don't let's say to ourselves, 'I have made such - and-such a number of prostrations, so now I have secured divine grace,' but rather let us make entreaty for the pure light of divine knowledge to shine within us and open our spiritual eyes so that we may understand His divine words.
In this way, without realizing it, we love God without contorting ourselves and without exertion and struggle. What is difficult for man is easy for God. We will love God suddenly when grace overshadows us. If we love Christ very much, the prayer will say itself. Christ will be continually in our mind and in our heart.
St. Porphyrios

Thirst after Jesus and He will satisfy you with His love.
St. Isaac the Syrian

You don't become holy by fighting evil. Let evil be
Look towards Christ and that will save you. What
makes a person saintly is love.
 St. Porphyrios

The fact that I am a monk and you are a layman is o
no importance. The Lord listens equally to the monk
and to the man of the world provided both are true
believers. He looks for a heart full of true faith into
which to send His Spirit. For the heart of a man is
capable of containing the Kingdom of God. The Holy
Spirit and the Kingdom of God are one.
St. Seraphim of Sarov

The enemy will run like a wild ass from the man who
has tasted the sweetness of prayer.
Elder Cleopas of Romania

Take heed often to come together to give thanks to
God and show forth His praise. For when you
assemble frequently in the same place, the powers of
Satan are destroyed, and the destruction at which he
aims is prevented by the unity of your faith. Nothing
is more precious than peace, by which all war, in
heaven and earth, is brought to an end.
St. Ignatius of Antioch

Concerning prayer in church, know that it is higher
than prayers at home, for it is raised by a whole

group of people, among which many are most pure prayers, offering to God from humble hearts, which He accepts as fragrant incense. Along with these our prayers are also accepted, even though they are feeble and worthless.
St. Macarius of Optina

Prayer frees the mind of all thought of the sensory and raises it to God Himself, Who is above all, to converse with Him and daringly ask Him for anything. Thus a man spends his life in purity, as one who, having already experienced communion with God, is thereupon again preparing for this communion.
St. Nilus of Sinai

Be mindful of God at all times, in all places, and in every circumstance. For no matter what you do, you should keep in mind the Creator of all things. When you see the light, do not forget Him who gave it to you; when you see the sky, the earth, the sea and all that is in them, marvel at these things and glorify their Creator; when you put on clothing, acknowledge whose gift it is and praise Him who in His providence has given you life. In short, if everything you do becomes for you an occasion for glorifying God, you will be praying unceasingly. And in this way your soul will always rejoice, as St. Paul commends (cf. I Thess. 5:16).
St. Peter of Damascus

When you are about to pray to our Lady the Holy Virgin, be firmly assured, before praying, that you will not depart from her without having received mercy. To think thus and to have confidence in her is meet and right. She is, the All-Merciful Mother of the All-Merciful God, the Word, and her mercies, incalculably great and innumerable, have been declared from all ages by all Christian Churches; she is, indeed, an abyss of mercies and bounties.
St. John of Kronstadt

When you look at the candles and lamps burning in church, rise in thought from the material fire to the immaterial fire of the Holy Ghost, for our God is a consuming fire. When you see and smell the fragrant incense, rise in thought to the spiritual fragrance of the Holy Ghost, 'for we are unto God a sweet savour of Christ.'
St. John of Kronstadt

Prayer is food for the soul. Do not starve the soul, it is better to let the body go hungry. Do not judge anyone, forgive everyone. Consider yourself worse than everyone in the world and you will be saved. As much as possible, be more quiet.
St. Joseph of Optina

Before the war begins, seek after your ally; before you fall ill, seek out your physician; and before grievous things come upon you, pray, and in the time of your

tribulations you will find Him, and He will listen to you.
St. Isaac the Syrian

Do not spare yourself, but pray earnestly, even if you have been toiling all day. Do not be negligent in holy prayer; say it to God unto the end from your whole heart, for it is a duty you owe to God.
St. John of Kronstadt

Do not let pass any opportunity to pray for anyone, either at his request or at the request of his relatives, friends, of those who esteem him, or of his acquaintances. The Lord looks favorably upon the prayer of our love, and upon our boldness before Him. Besides this, prayer for others is very beneficial to the one himself who prays for others; it purifies the heart, strengthens faith and hope in God, and enkindles our love for God and our neighbor. When praying, say thus: 'Lord, it is possible for Thee to do this or that to this servant of Thine; do this for him, for Thy name is the Merciful Love of Men and the Almighty.'
St. John of Kronstadt

Sometimes people call prayer that which is not prayer at all; for instance: a man goes to church, stands there for a time, looks at the icons or at other people, their faces and dress, and says that he has prayed to God; or else he stands before an icon at

home, bows his head, says some words he has learnt by heart, without understanding and without feeling and says that he has prayed, although with his thoughts and heart he has not prayed at all, but was elsewhere with other people and things, and not with God.
St. John of Kronstadt

It is this war of attention and prayer on which both life and death of the soul depend. By attention that we keep our prayer safe and therefore we progress: if we do not have attention to keep it clear and we leave it unguarded, then it is inflected by evil thoughts and we become wicked and hopeless.
St. Symeon the New Theologian

Because when we say, "Thy will be done," and wholly surrender ourselves to God, it is then that the will of God is indeed done. But we, on one hand, say, "Thy will be done," and on the other hand, keep persisting in our own will. Well, what is God supposed to do then?
St. Paisios of Mount Athos

Do not be foolish in the requests you make to God otherwise you will insult God through your ignorance. Act wisely in prayer, so that you may become worthy of glorious things. Ask for things that are honourable from Him Who will not hold back, so that you may receive honour from Him as a result of

the wise choice your free will had made. Solomon asked for wisdom (3 Kg 3:8-14) – and along with it he also received the earthly kingdom, for he knew how to ask wisely of the heavenly King, that is, for things that are important.
St. Isaac the Syrian

Sometimes during a lengthy prayer only a few minutes are really pleasing to God, and constitute true prayer, true service to Him. The chief thing in prayer is the nearness of the heart to God.
St. John of Kronstadt

He who prays for others prays for himself.
St. Basil the Great

Prayer is a request for what is good, offered by the devout of God. But we do not restrict this request simply to what is stated in words. We should not express our prayer merely in syllables, but the power of prayer should be expressed in the moral attitude of our soul and in the virtuous actions that extend throughout our life... This is how you pray continually — not by offering prayer in words, but by joining yourself to God through your whole way of life, so that your life becomes one continuous and uninterrupted prayer.
St Basil the Great

A psalm is the work of angels, a heavenly institution,

the spiritual incense.
St. Basil the Great

Let your prayer be completely simple. For both the
publican and the prodigal son were reconciled to God
by a single phrase.
St. John Climacus

Do not say, after spending a long time in prayer, that
nothing has been gained; for you have already gained
something. And what higher good is there than to
cling to the Lord and persevere in unceasing union
with Him?
St. John Climacus

The first stage of this tranquility consists in silencing
the lips when the heart is excited. The second, in
silencing the mind when the soul is still excited. The
goal is a perfect peacefulness even in the middle of
the raging storm.
St. John Climacus

Always remember God and your mind will become
Heaven.
St. Nilos the Wise

If you pray at night and are not careful with your
lifestyle during the day, it is as though you are
building and destroying at the same time.
Elder Ephraim of Mount Athos and Arizona

Appetite comes from eating and prayer from praying.
Elder Ephraim of Mount Athos and Arizona

When you are weary of praying, and dost not receive, consider how often you have heard a poor man calling upon you, and hast not listened to him, and he has not been angry nor insulted you.
St. John Chrysostom

Let not one think, my fellow Christian, that only priests and monks need to pray without ceasing and not laymen No, no; every Christian without exception ought to dwell always in prayer.
St. Gregory of Palamas

Prayer changes from entreaty to thanksgiving and meditation on the divine truths of faith fills the heart with a sense of jubilation and unimpeachable hope. This hope is a foretaste of future blessings, of which the soul even now receives direct experience, and so it comes to know in part the surpassing richness of God's bounty, in accordance with the Psalmist's words, 'Taste and know that the Lord is bountiful' (Ps. 34:8). For He is the jubilation of the righteous, the joy of the upright, the gladness of the humble, and the solace of those who grieve because of Him.
St. Gregory Palamas

What a man thinks and feels as he prays to God is

more important to God than the words his tongue forms. The tongue is capable of delusion, but the heart does not delude: it shows a man as he is - black or white.
St. Nikolai Velimirovich

When guided by prayer, the moral powers within us become stronger than all our temptations and conquer them.
Elder Ephraim of Arizona

Do not abandon prayer until you see that, by Divine providence, fervour and tears have diminished. For perhaps you will not have such a moment for the remission of your sins again in your life.
St. John Climacus

He who abandons prayer abandons his salvation; he who is careless about prayer is careless about his salvation; he who quits prayer renounces his salvation.
St. Ignatius Brianchaninov

If you do not cut off the inner flow of evil thoughts by prayer and humility, but fight against them merely with the weapon of fasting and bodily hardship, you will labour in vain. But if through prayer and humility you sanctify the root you will attain outward sanctity as well.
St. Gregory Palamas

Men can attain to holiness only in God, not by nature, but by participation, by struggle, by prayer.
St. Cyril of Jerusalem

A Father asked his elder how to pray and the elder said to him, "First pray with your mouth, because from the mouth the prayer passes to the mind and then to the heart. And for this we need much labour, many tears, and the grace of the Holy Spirit."
St. Cleopas of Romania

A disciple asked his elder "What is pure prayer?"
"To speak with the mouth, to understand it with the mind, and to feel it with the heart," the elder replied.
St. Cleopas of Romania

The more you pray and entreat God for your sins, the more the evil demons withdraw from you; while the more you neglect prayer and lack the desire to pray, the more they approach you and you become their dwelling place.
Elder Gabriel Dionysiotis

We have two powerful weapons which the devil fears and which make him tremble: first, we have the sign of the cross applied with faith in our crucified Christ, and second, with the sign of the cross we also have the sweetest name of Jesus pronounced prayerfully and sensibly by the lips from the depths of the heart.

Elder Athanasius of Ploschonsk

Virtues are formed by prayer. Prayer preserves temperance. Prayer suppresses anger. Prayer prevents emotions of pride and envy. Prayer draws into the soul the Holy Spirit, and raises man to Heaven.
St. Ephraim of Syria

The enchanter knoweth not the power of the words which he uttereth, but when the animal heareth them it knoweth their power, and he become subservient and submitteth itself (to him). Even so is it with us for although we do not know the power of the words whereon we meditate, the devils know their power as soon as they hear them.
Abba Poemen

As two words cannot be uttered at the same time by one voice, and be recognised and understood, so it is with a mixed prayer uttered by man before God.
Sayings of the Desert Fathers

The beginning of the path to pure prayer is the battle against the passions. There can be no progress in prayer while the passions are active.
St. Joseph the Hesychast

Prayer is the language of the age to come.
St. Joseph the Hesychast.

Prayer for enemies is the climax of the rational perfection of beings in whom what is mortal is swallowed up by life.
St. Joseph the Hesychast

Miserable are those among the dead for whom none of the living prays.
St. John of Damascus

Stand with awareness and attention in the heart, pronounce ceaselessly "Lord Jesus Christ, Son of God, have mercy on me a sinner," without picturing any sort of image or face, but with faith that the Lord will see and attend to you.
St. Theophan the Recluse

If you do not feel like praying, you have to force yourself. The Holy Fathers say that prayer with force is higher than unforced prayer. You do not want to, but force yourself. The Kingdom of Heaven is taken by force (Mt. 11 v12).
St. Ambrose of Optina

Every virtue, from practice, becomes a habit, but one must force oneself in prayer to one's very death. It is opposed by our "old man", and the enemy especially rises up against one who prays. Prayer Is the insinuation of death to the devil; it defeats him. Even the saints, such as St. Seraphim, had to force

themselves in prayer, not to mention us sinners.
St. Barsanuphius of Optina

Prayer in church is important. The best thoughts and
feelings come in church, yes, and the enemy attacks
more violently in church, but with the sign of the
Cross and the Jesus Prayer, you drive him away. It is
good to stand in some dark corner in church and to
pray to God. "Let us lift up our hearts!" the priest
exclaims, but our mind often creeps along the ground
thinking about indecent things. Fight against this.
St. Barsanuphius of Optina

Intending to offer up your prayer to God, cast aside all
earthly thoughts and cares. Do not engage in the
thoughts which come to you at that time, however
important or brilliant or necessary they might seem.
Render to God the things that are God's and you will
have time to render what is necessary for temporal
life in its own time.
St. Igantius Brianchaninov

A false understanding or conception of prayer always
leads to a fruitless or harmful practice of it.
St. Ignatius Brianchaninov

In short, let every action be a cause of your
remembering and praising God, and lo! You will be
praying without ceasing and therein your soul will
always rejoice.

St. Peter of Damascus

The Jesus Prayer is work common to angels and humans.

With this prayer people attain to the life of the angels in a short time.

The prayer is the source of all good works and virtues and drives the dark passions far away from man.

In a short time it makes a man capable of acquiring the grace of the Holy Spirit.

Acquire it, and before you die you will have acquired an angelic soul.

The prayer is divine rejoicing.

No other spiritual weapon can so effectively restrain the demons.

It burns them as fire burns a wick.

St. Paisius Velichkovsky

Love Of God

Let no one deceive you, brother: without holiness, as the apostle says, no one can see God (Heb. 12:14).

For the Lord, who is more than holy and beyond all purity, will not appear to an impure person.

Just as he who loves father or mother, daughter or son (Matt. 10:37) more than the Lord is unworthy of Him, so is he who loves anything transient and material.

Even more unworthy is the person who chooses foul and fetid sin to preference to love for the Lord; for God rejects whoever does not repudiate all filthiness: 'Corruption does not inherit incorruption' (1 Cor 15:50). "

St. Theognostos

That which a man loves, to which he turns, that he will find. If he loves earthly things, he will find earthly things, and these earthly things will abide in his heart will communicate their earthliness to him and will find him; if he loves heavenly things, he will find heavenly things, and they will abide in his heart and give him life.

St. John of Kronstadt

With sincere Christians prayer is continual gratitude, because we continually sin; gratitude is perpetual, because every day, every moment we receive fresh mercies from God, besides the old mercies which are numberless. Praise is also perpetual, because we perpetually see the glory of our God's works in ourselves and in the world, especially the glory of His infinite love to us.

St. John of Kronstadt

When Christ is in our heart, we are contented with everything: what has been discomfort to us becomes the greatest comfort, what was bitter to us becomes sweet, poverty becomes wealth, our hunger is satisfied, and our sorrow turns into joy!

St. John of Kronstadt

Do not cling with your heart to anything, and do not make it the god of your heart; the sole God of our heart must be the Lord-God, Who created it: for our heart is His breath.

Do not cleave with your whole heart unto any person, that is to any flesh, for the sole God of our heart must be the Lord-God, and to Him only must we cleave. For attachment to material things, or to flesh, is a lie, an enticement of Satan and the will of the Devil. Amen.

St. John of Kronstadt

To love Christ means not to be a hireling, not to look upon a noble life as an enterprise or trade, but to be a

true benefactor and to do everything only for the sake of love for God.
St. John Chrysostom

If a musician, or a dancer, or anyone else connected with the theatre should summon them to the city they all hurry eagerly, and thank the one who invited them, and spend an entire half-day with their attention fixed on the performer exclusively. Yet when God addresses us through the prophets and apostles, we yawn, we are bored, we become drowsy.
St. John Chrysostom

For if we refrain from sin merely out of fear of punishment, it is quite clear that, unless punishment had awaited us, we should have done things deserving punishment, since our propensity is for sinning. But if we abstain from evil actions not through threat of punishment, but because we hate such actions, then it is from love of the Master that we practice the virtues, fearful lest we should fall away from Him.
St. Theodoros the Great Ascetic

He who has realized love for God in his heart is tireless, as Jeremiah says, in his pursuit of the Lord his God, and bears every hardship, reproach and insult nobly, never thinking the least evil of anyone.
St. Maximos the Confessor

God created everything not only for our use, but also that we, seeing the great wealth of His creations, might be astonished at the might of the Creator and might understand that all this was created with wisdom and unutterable goodness for the honour of man, who was to appear.
St. John Chrysostom

Blessed is he who strives to please the Lord as others try to please men.
St. John Climacus

The Lord wants us to love one another. Here is freedom: in love for God and neighbour. In this freedom, there is equality. In earthly orders, there may not be equality, but this is not important for the soul. Not everyone can be a king, not everyone a patriarch or a boss. But in any position it is possible to love God and to please Him, and only this is important. And whoever loves God more on earth will be in greater glory in His Kingdom.
St. Silouan the Athonite

Let us hold fast to love of Christ, hating and rightly turning away from the devil. For as our benefactor is loved and cherished in proportion to his benefactions, so the wicked one should be hated and rejected for his ways in equal proportion. For he is the destroyer of our life. In the words of the Master, he is a murderer from the beginning [John 8:44]. He is

the one who has divided our race into ten thousand opinions, wounding it with many darts of sin and seeking to swallow down the inhabited world. If we do not hate him, there will be no escaping the punishment that will be meted out to us, because we joined to our foe and murderer. But, my brothers, let us fly from him! Let us fly most certainly. What is flight? The avoidance of wicked actions and thoughts, and also affinity with God, the assumption of good works.
St. Theodore the Studite

The wondrous God-man, is the 'one thing that is needed' (Luke 10:42) by man in all his worlds and in his every life. Therefore, only the God-man is justified in asking of us that which no one else has ever dared to ask: that we love Him more than we love parents, siblings, children, friends, the earth, the angels, anyone and everyone in all the worlds, visible and invisible (Matth. 10:37-39; Luke 14:26, Rom. 8 31-39).
St. Justin Popovich

Put Christ first because He puts us first, and let nothing deter us from loving Him.
St. Cyprian of Carthage

To deny oneself means to give up one's bad habits; to root out of the heart all that ties us to the world; not to cherish bad thoughts or desires; to suppress every

evil thought; not to desire to do anything out of self - love, but to do everything out of love for God.
St. Innocent of Alaska

When you sit down to eat, pray. When you eat bread, do so thanking Him for being so generous to you. If you drink wine, be mindful of Him who has given it to you for your pleasure and as a relief in sickness. When you dress, thank Him for His kindness in providing you with clothes. When you look at the sky and the beauty of the stars, throw yourself at God's feet and adore Him who in His wisdom has arranged things in this way. Similarly, when the sun goes down and when it rises, when you are asleep or awake, give thanks to God, who created and arranged all things for your benefit, to have you know, love and praise their Creator.
St. Basil the Great

We must begin with thanksgiving for everything. The beginning of joy is to be content with your situation.
St. Ambrose of Optina

God is everywhere. There is no place God is not...You cry out to Him, 'Where art Thou, my God?' And He answers, "I am present, my child! I am always beside you." Both inside and outside, above and below, wherever you turn, everything shouts, 'God!' In Him we live and move. We breathe God, we eat God, we clothe ourselves with God. Everything praises and blesses God. All of creation shouts His praise. Everything animate and inanimate speaks wondrously and glorifies the Creator. Let every breath praise the Lord!

St. Joseph the Hesychast

Repentance

Christian perfection consists of holiness—that is, freedom of the soul from enslavement to sin. It stands to reason that all people without exception, not only priests or monastics, are called to this perfection or holiness that consists of freedom from sin.
Archbishop Averky (Taushev)

Because happiness in both this world and the next consists of doing God's will, the Holy Fathers, as experts in the spiritual life, beckon us to pay careful attention to our conscience. If we do so, they tell us, then it will reliably and precisely show us the clear and direct will of God. They term this the "guarding of one's conscience."
Archbishop Averky (Taushev)

The forgetting of wrongs is a sign of true repentance. But he who dwells on them and thinks that he is repenting is like a man who thinks he is running while he is really asleep.
St. John Climacus

If we judged ourselves we would not be judged.
1 Corinthians 11 v.13

Through repentance the filth of our foul actions is washed away. After this, we participate in the Holy Spirit, not automatically, but according to the faith humility and inner disposition of the repentance in which our soul is engaged. For this reason it is good to repent each day as the act of repentance is unending.

St. Symeon the New Theologian

When our soul leaves this world we shall not be blamed for not having worked miracles, or for not having been theologians, or not having been rapt in divine visions. But we shall certainly have to give an account to God of why we have not unceasingly mourned.

St. John Climacus

Mourning is the conditional pain of a soul on fire.

St. John Climacus

The Church is holy, although there are sinners within her. Those who sin, but who cleanse themselves with true repentance, do not keep the Church from being holy. But unrepentant sinners are cut off, whether visibly by Church authority, or invisibly by the judgement of God, from the body of the Church. And so in this regard the Church remains holy.

St. Philaret of Moscow

The time of this life is for repentance; the very fact that a sinner still lives is a pledge that God will accept whoever desires to return to Him.
St. Gregory Palamas

Pay attention carefully. After the sin comes the shame; courage follows repentance. Did you pay attention to what I said? Satan upsets the order; he gives the courage to sin and the shame to repentance.
St. John Chrysostom

Do not be ashamed to enter again into the Church. Be ashamed when you sin. Do not be ashamed when you repent. Pay attention to what the devil did to you. These are two things: sin and repentance. Sin is a wound; repentance is a medicine. Just as there are for the body wounds and medicines, so for the soul are sins and repentance. However, sin has the shame and repentance possesses the courage.
St. John Chrysostom

Enter into the Church and wash away your sins. For here is a hospital for sinners and not a court of law,
St. John Chrysostom

There are five baptisms. First is Moses', when the Hebrews passed over the Red Sea. Second, that of John the Baptist. Third, that of our Lord Jesus Christ, without which baptism one is not a Christian. Fourth, martyrdom: baptism in blood. Christ suffered this

baptism. And fifth, the baptism of tears, which comes from the remembrance of one's sins. Do all in your will not to fall, for the strong athlete should not fall. But if you do fall, get up again at once and continue the contest. Even if you fall a thousand times, rise up again each time, and keep doing this until the day of your death.
St. John of Karpathos

Years are not needed for true repentance, and no days, but only an instant.
St. Ambrose of Optina

If you wish to be in control of your soul and body, forestall the passions by rooting out their causes.
St. Thalassios the Libyan

There will be a judgement, and it will be shame and fear without hope. Shame and fear at confession pay for the shame and fear then. If you do not want the latter, go through with the former.
St. Theophan the Recluse

If you have sinned, acknowledge the sin and repent, God will forgive the sin and once again give you a new heart...and a new spirit (Ez. 36:26). There is no other way: Either do not sin, or repent.
St. Theophan the Recluse

If you wish, you can be a slave of passions, and if you

wish, you can remain free and not submit to their yoke; for God has created you with that power.
St. Anthony the Great

Place your sins before you and look through them to God.
St. Anthony the Great

In the words of the psalmist, 'As you lie in bed, repent of what you say in your heart' (Ps. 4:4 LXX), that is, repent in the stillness of the night, remembering the lapses that occurred in the confusion of the day and disciplining yourself in hymns and spiritual songs (Col. 3:16) – in other words, teaching yourself to persist in prayer and psalmody through attentive meditation on what you read. For the practice of the moral virtues is effectuated by meditating on what has happened during the day, so that during the stillness of the night we can become aware of the sins we have committed and can grieve over them.
St. Peter of Damascus

Even if you are not what you should be, you should not despair. It is bad enough that you have sinned; why in addition do you wrong God by regarding Him in your ignorance as powerless? Is He, who for your sake created the great universe that you behold, incapable of saving your soul? And if you say that this fact, as well as His incarnation, only makes your condemnation worse, then repent; and He will

receive your repentance, as He accepted that of the prodigal son (Luke 15:20) and the prostitute (Luke 7:37-50). But if repentance is too much for you, and you sin out of habit even when you do not want to, show humility like the publican (Luke 18:13): this is enough to ensure your salvation. For he who sins without repenting, yet does not despair, must of necessity regard himself as the lowest of creatures, and will not dare to judge or censure anyone. Rather, he will marvel at God's compassion.
St. Peter of Damascus

Let us be neither hasty nor tardy, and let us be always ready to make a new start. If you fall, rise up. If you fall again, rise up again. Only do not abandon your Physician, lest you be condemned as worse than a suicide because of your despair. Wait on Him, and He will be merciful, either reforming you, or sending you trials, or through some other provision of which you are ignorant.
St. Peter of Damascus

Every day before you go to sleep, make a private confession to the Lord of everything in which you have sinned. Lying down to sleep is like departing for the other world.
St. Theophan the Recluse

Wounds shown to the doctor do not get worse but are healed.

St. John Climacus

Psalmody is a weapon, prayer a wall, and pure tears a cleansing bath.
St. John Climacus

There is no confession of sins at any time except in this present life. By his own will each man is permitted, and has throughout his life, the freedom to choose repentance. But when we die we lose life and along with it the right to exercise our will.
St. Hilary De Poitiers

Wherefore on no account suffer any evil habit to master thee; but, while it is yet young, pluck the evil root out of thine heart, lest it fasten on and strike root so deep that time and labour be required to uproot it.
St. John of Damascus

A soldier asked Abba Mius if God accepted repentance. After the old man had taught him many things he said: "Tell me, if your cloak is torn do you throw it away?"
He replied, "No, I mend it and use it again."
The old man said to him, "If you are so careful about your cloak, will not God be equally careful about His creature?"
Sayings of the Desert Fathers

With all diligence ask the Lord for the greatest and

most needful of all gifts — to see your own sins and cry over them. He who has this gift has everything.
Abbot Nikon Vorobiev

In spite of our sinfulness, in spite of the darkness surrounding our souls, the Grace of the Holy Spirit conferred by baptism in the name of the Father and the Son and the Holy Spirit, still shines in our heart with the inextinguishable light of Christ ... and when the sinner turns to the way of repentance the light smooths away every trace of the sins committed clothing the former sinner in the garments of incorruption, spun of the Grace of the Holy Spirit. It is this acquisition of the Holy Spirit about which I have been speaking.
St. Seraphim of Sarov

Beguiling and deceptive is the life of the world fruitless its labour, perilous its delight, poor its riches delusive its honours, inconstant, insignificant; and woe to those who hope in its seeming goods: because of this many die without repentance.
Elder Nazarius

Maintain the conviction that our disorderliness is not natural to us, and do not listen to those who say, 'It is no use talking about it, because that is just how we are made, and you cannot do anything about it.' That is not how we are made, and if we undertake to cure ourselves, then we will be able to do something about

it.
St. Theophan the Recluse

An evident sinner will turn towards good more easily than a secret sinner, hiding under the cloak of visible virtues.
St. Theophan the Recluse

The saints were people like all of us. Many of them came out of great sins, but by repentance they attained the Kingdom of Heaven. And everyone who comes there comes through repentance, which the merciful Lord has given us through His sufferings.
St. Silouan the Athonite

Struggle with all your power to gain Paradise. And do not listen to those who say that everyone will be saved. This is a trap of Satan so that we won't struggle.
St. Paisios of Mt. Athos

It is impossible not to often fall into sin unless you have a hatred of it implanted in your heart. Self-love must be eradicated. Every sin comes from the love of self. Sin always appears, or feigns to be, to wish us well, promising us plenteousness and ease. 'The tree was good for food, and it was pleasant to the eyes, and a tree to be desired to make one wise.' (Genesis 3:6) This is how sin always appears to us.
St. John of Kronstadt

As the Searcher of hearts, the Lord knows that men are liable to very frequently trespass, and that, having fallen, they often rise up again; therefore He has given us the commandment to frequently forgive trespasses, and He Himself is the first to fulfil His holy word. As soon as you say from your whole heart, 'repent,' you will be immediately forgiven.
St. John of Kronstadt

The sick one who is acquainted with his sickness is easily to be cured; and he who confesses his pain is near to health.
Many are the pains of the hard heart; and when the sick one resists the physician, his torments will be augmented.
St. Isaac the Syrian

According to Thy mercy, pour out upon me, who am miserable, at least one small drop of grace to make me understand and be converted, that I might make at least some small effort to correct myself. For if Thy grace does not illumine my soul, I will not be able to see the carelessness and negligence that the passions have produced in me through my apathy and recklessness.
St. Ephraim the Syrian

God is loving to man, and loving in no small measure. For say not, I have committed fornication an adultery: I have done dreadful things, and not once only, but often: will He forgive? Will He grant pardon? Hear what the Psalmist says: How great is the multitude of Your goodness, O Lord!

Your accumulated offenses surpass not the multitude of God's mercies: your wounds surpass not the great Physician's skill. Only give yourself up in faith: tell the Physician your ailment: say thou also, like David: I said, I will confess me my sin unto the Lord: and the same shall be done in your case, which he says immediately: And you forgave the wickedness of my heart.

St. Cyril of Jerusalem

The woman who purposely destroys her unborn child is guilty of murder. With us there is no nice inquiry as to its being formed or unformed. In this case it is not only the being about to be born who is vindicated, but the woman in her attack upon herself; because in most cases women who make such attempts die. The destruction of the embryo is an additional crime, a second murder, at all events if we regard it as done with intent. The punishment, however, of these women should not be for life, but for the term of ten years. And let their treatment depend not on mere lapse of time, but on the character of their repentance.

St. Basil the Great

Repentance without fasting is idle.

St. Basil the Great

Holiness

Those who keep the gates of the Kingdom of Heaven, if they do not see in a Christian the likeness of Christ, as a son to his father, will by no means open them to him and allow him to enter.
St. Symeon the New Theologian

The rule of life for a perfect person is to be in the image and likeness of God.
St. Clement of Alexandria

God does not come near to where flesh is in charge: God's contact with man is through his spirit, and the spirit in such a person is out of its proper order. He will feel God's calling for the first time when his spirit begins to claim its rights in the voice of conscience and the fear of God. And when a man finally makes his free deliberate choice for the spirit, then God will join that man and dwell in him. From that moment on begins the conversion of his soul and body, the whole inner and outer man, until "God may be all in all" (1 Cor. 15:28), and the man which once was carnal, transforms into a spiritual being and becomes sanctified. What a marvelous privilege of mankind, and how few of us know about it, appreciate it and

seek it!
St. Theophan the Recluse

The Word is our master and we must be imitators of His works and doers of His word.
St. Irenaeus

It is not what man does which counts in eternal life but what he is; whether he is like Jesus Christ, our Lord, or if he is different and unlike Him.
St. Symeon the New Theologian

Perfection is clearly not achieved simply by being naked, by the lack of wealth or by the rejection of honours, unless there is also that love whose ingredients the apostle described (I Cor. 13) and which is to be found solely in purity of heart. Not to be jealous, not to be puffed up, not to act heedlessly, not to seek what does not belong to one, not to rejoice over some injustice, not to plan evil - what is this and its like if not the continuous offering to God of the heart that is perfect and truly pure, a heart kept free of all disturbance?
St. John Cassian

If there is any rest for us in this world, then it consists only in purity of the conscience and patience. This is harbour for us who sail upon the sea of life.
St. Tikhon of Zadonsk

No wonder, then, that it is so hard to be Christian — it is not hard it is impossible. No one can knowingly accept a way of life which, the more truly it is lived, leads more surely to one's own destruction. And that is why we constantly rebel, try to make life easier, try to be half-Christian, try to make the best of both worlds. We must ultimately choose — our felicity lies in one world or the other, not in both.
Father Seraphim Rose

It is a great art to succeed in having your soul sanctified. A person can become a saint anywhere. He can become a saint in Omonia Square, if he wants. At your work, whatever it may be, you can become a saint through meekness, patience, and love. Make a new start every day, with new resolution, with enthusiasm and love, prayer and silence - not with anxiety so that you get a pain in the chest.
St. Porphyrios

Let no one deceive you, brother: without holiness, as the apostle says, no one can see God (Heb. 12:14).
For the Lord, who is more than holy and beyond all purity, will not appear to an impure person.
Just as he who loves father or mother, daughter or son (Matt. 10:37) more than the Lord is unworthy of Him, so is he who loves anything transient and material.
Even more unworthy is the person who chooses foul and fetid sin to preference to love for the Lord; for

God rejects whoever does not repudiate all filthiness. 'Corruption does not inherit incorruption' (1 Cor 15:50)."
St. Theognostos

The only hope of salvation from the delusions and the heresies, the innovations and the traps of wicked people and of the devil is prayer, repentance and humility.
St. Joseph the Hesychast

God seeks three things from the baptised: from the soul – genuine faith; from the body – self-restraint and from the tongue – truth.
St. Gregory the Theologian

When God revealed Himself, He united Himself with our mortal nature in order to deify humanity through this close relation with deity. Since this is so, through His flesh, constituted by bread and wine, He implants Himself in all believers.
St. Gregory of Nyssa

Every Christian should find for himself the imperative and incentive to become holy. If you live without struggle and without hope of becoming holy, then you are Christians only in name and not in essence. But without holiness, no one shall see the Lord, that is to say they will not attain eternal blessedness. It is trustworthy saying that Jesus Christ came into the

world to save sinners (1 Tim. 1:15). But we deceive ourselves if we think that we are saved while remaining sinners. Christ saves those sinners by giving them the means to become saints.
St. Philaret of Moscow

One must clean the royal house from every impurity and adorn it with every beauty, then the king may enter into it. In a similar way one must first cleanse the earth of the heart and uproot the weeds of sin and the passionate deeds and soften it with sorrows and the narrow way of life, sow in it the seed of virtue, water it with lamentation and tears, and only then does the fruit of dispassion and eternal life grow. For the Holy Spirit does not dwell in a man until he has been cleansed from passions of the soul and body.
St. Paisius Velichkovsky

Whether we think, speak or act in a good or an evil manner depends upon whether we cleave inwardly to virtue or to vice.
St. Thalassios the Libyan

As the Lord put on the body, leaving behind all principality and power, so Christians put on the Holy Spirit, and are at rest.
St. Macarius the Great

That Paradise was closed and a Cherubim was commanded to prevent man from entering it by a flaming sword: of this we believe that in visible fashion it was indeed just as it is written, and at the same time we find that this occurs mystically in every soul.

St. Marcarius the Great

To become completely holy, both in soul and in body, that is our vocation. This is not a miracle, but rather the norm, the rule of faith. The commandment of the Holy Gospel is clear and most clear: as the Holy One who has called you is Holy, so be ye holy in all manner of life (1 Peter 1:15).

St. Justin Popovich

The consumption of the Body of Christ becomes beneficial when in spirit we strive towards Him and unite ourselves with Him. Receiving the Body of Christ, while turning away from Him in spirit, is like the contact with Christ which they had who struck Him and mocked and crucified Him. Their contact with Him served not for their salvation and healing but for their condemnation.

But those who partake with piety, love and readiness to serve Him, closely unite themselves with Him and become instruments of His Divine will.

St. John of Shanghai

The holy canons dictate that Christians should spend the eves of feast days in prayer and with reverence in preparation for participation or attendance at the

Divine Liturgy. If all Orthodox Christians are called to this, then this pertains all the more to those who take an active part in the church services itself. Their participation in diversions on the eve of a feast day is especially sinful. In view of the above, those who attend a dance or similar form of entertainment and diversion may not participate in the choir the next day, may not serve in the altar, enter the altar or stand on the cliros.
St. John of Shanghai

The Church, through the temple and Divine service, acts upon the entire man, educates him wholly; acts upon his sight, hearing, smelling, feeling, taste, imagination, mind, and will, by the splendour of the icons and of the whole temple, by the ringing of bells, by the singing of the choir, by the fragrance of the incense, the kissing of the Gospel, of the cross and the holy icons, by the prosphoras, the singing, and sweet sound of the readings of the Scriptures.
St. John of Kronstadt

Fear evil like fire. Don't let it touch your heart, even if it seems just or righteous. No matter what the circumstances, don't let it come into you. Evil is always evil.
St. John of Kronstadt

Everything that breathes, breathes by air and cannot live without air; similarly all reasonable free

creatures live by the Holy Spirit, as though by air, and cannot live without Him. "Every soul is quickened by the Holy Spirit." Recognize that the Holy Spirit stands in the same relation to your soul as air stands in relation to your body.
St. John of Kronstadt

Correct faith does not benefit in anything when life is corrupted.
St. John Chrysostom

When we teach children to be good, to be gentle, to be forgiving (all these are attributes of God), to be generous, to love their fellow men, to regard this present age as nothing, we instil virtue in their souls and reveal the image of God within them.
St John Chrysostom

Let us become like Christ, since Christ became like us. Let us become Divine for His sake, since for us He became Man.
He assumed the worse that He might give us the better. He became poor that by His poverty we might become rich. He accepted the form of a servant that we might win back our freedom.
St Gregory the Theologian

The Doctor of our souls has placed the remedy in the hidden regions of the soul.
St. John Cassian

The women who came with spices saw angels, since those who advance toward God through their holy desires, accompanied by the sweet smell of the virtues, behold the citizens from on high.
St. Gregory the Great

Death

In the depths of each person's heart lies the knowledge of his immortality. And he is indeed immortal, and that which we call death is a birth into a new life, a transition from one state of being to another.
Abbot Nikon Vorobiev

You must not be greatly troubled about many things but you should care for the main thing - preparing yourself for death.
St. Ambrose of Optina

Many of our departed neighbours, especially those who reposed without proper preparation, need our help incomparably more than those among the living who are extremely impoverished, because the reposed are now incapable of helping themselves. Only we the living can offer help.
Metropolitan Gregory (Postnikov) of St. Petersburg

We see the water of a river flowing uninterruptedly and passing away, and all that floats on its surface, rubbish or beams of trees, all pass by. Christian! So does our life. . . I was an infant, and that time has

gone. I was an adolescent, and that too has passed. I was a young man, and that too is far behind me. The strong and mature man that I was is no more. My hair turns white, I succumb to age, but that too passes; I approach the end and will go the way of all flesh. I was born in order to die. I die that I may live. Remember me, O Lord, in Thy Kingdom!
St. Tikhon of Zadonsk

Our mind is so darkened by the fall that unless we force ourselves to remember death we can completely forget about it. When we forget about death, then we begin to live on earth as if we were immortal, and we sacrifice all our activity to the world without concerning ourselves in the least either about the fearful transition to eternity or about our fate in eternity. Then we boldly and peremptorily override the commandments of Christ; then we commit all the vilest sins; then we abandon not only unceasing prayer but even the prayers appointed for definite times -we begin to scorn this essential and indispensable occupation as if it were an activity of little importance and little needed. Forgetful of physical death, we die a spiritual death.
St. Ignatius Brianchaninov

Are you not afraid of death, which we shall all face in a little while? How are we to look on the fearsome angels, as they come to take us from the body? How are we to journey on that long and unending road, if

we have not obtained the necessities for the journey?
St. Theodore the Studite

Like the tax collectors who sit in the narrow roads and seize the passers-by and the oppressed, so also the demons watch carefully and grab hold of souls. And when they pass out of the body, if they are not completely purified, they are not permitted to go up into the mansions of Heaven there to meet their Master. For they are driven down by the demons of the air.
St. Macarius the Great

Our grief over the death of our close ones would be inconsolable and boundless if the Lord had not given us eternal life. Our life would be meaningless if it ended with death. What benefit, then, would there be from virtue or good deeds? They would be right who say, "Let us eat and drink, for tomorrow we die!" But man was created for immortality.
St. John of Shanghai

Truly most frightening is the mystery of death, how the soul is violently separated from its concord with the body and, by divine decree, the most natural bond of their cohesion is severed.
St. John Damascus

All who have lived according to God still live unto God, though they have departed this life. For this

reason, God is called the God of Abraham, Isaac and Jacob, since He is the God, not of the dead, but of the living (Mt. 22:32).
St. Gregory the Theologian

We needed an Incarnate God, a God put to death, that we might live. We were put to death together with Him, that we might be cleansed; we rose again with Him because we were put to death with Him; we were glorified with Him, because we rose again with Him.
St. Gregory the Theologian

While the dying person addresses his last words to us, suddenly his tongue is at a loss, his eyes dim, his mouth falls silent, his voice paralyzed when the Lord's troops have arrived, when His frightening armies overwhelm him, when the divine bailiffs invite the soul to be gone from the body, when the inexorable lays hold of us to drag us to the tribunal... Then the angels take the soul and go off through the air. There stand principalities, powers and leaders of the adverse troops who govern the world, merciless accusers, strict agents of an implacable tax bureau, like so many examiners that await the soul in the air, ready to demand a reckoning, to examine everything, brandishing their claims, that is to say our sins: those of youth and of old age, those intentional and those not so, those committed by actions and those by words or thoughts. Great then is the fear of the poor

soul, inexpressible its anguish when it sees itself at grips with these myriads of enemies, who stop it push and shove it, accuse it, hinder it from dwelling in the light, from entering into the land of the living. But the holy angels, taking the soul, lead it away.
St. Ephraim of Syria

If we make every effort to avoid death of the body, still more should it be our endeavour to avoid death of the soul. There is no obstacle for a man who wants to be saved other than negligence and laziness of soul.
St. Anthony the Great

It is later than you think! Hasten, therefore, to do the work of God.
Father Seraphim Rose

Courage

Even if we find ourselves with the devil or amongst wild beasts, God is present. Neither the devil nor wild beasts are able to harm us if they do not have the authority from God to do so.
Elder Ephraim of Mount Athos and Arizona

Struggle Mightily. Do not fear, for we have before us our big brothers – the angels – who fight together with us. They are incomparably stronger than the demons. Therefore, take courage. Strengthen yourselves with true self-knowledge, for the truth protects a struggler like a mighty weapon.
Elder Ephraim of Mount Athos and Arizona

He who has become the servant of the Lord will fear his Master alone, but he who does not yet fear Him is often afraid of his own shadow.
St. John Climacus

The labour of every struggle passes, but the victory remains.
Elder Ephraim of Mount Athos and Arizona

One must guard against complaining, as though it

were a poisonous snake.
Abbot Nikon Vorobiev

You see people abusing and reviling holy and sacred things and others not saying anything. Being meek on such an occasion is demonic.
St. Paisios of Mount Athos

It is preferable for a sensitive person to die once out of love in order to protect his neighbour, rather than be neglectful or cowardly and then to be constantly tormented by his conscience for the rest of his life.
St. Paisios of Mount Athos

When despair attacks us let us not yield to it, but being strengthened and protected by the light of faith with great courage let us say to the evil spirit: "What are you to us, estranged from God, a fugitive from heaven and evil servant? You dare do nothing to us, Christ, the Son of God, has authority both over us and over everything. It is against Him that we have sinned, and before Him that we will be justified. And you, destroyer, leave us. Strengthen by His venerable Cross, we trample under foot your serpent's head" (St. Antioch, Discourse 27).
St. Seraphim of Sarov

In our age of moral and spiritual decline, only the heroic example of righteous men and women is able to ignite a zeal for godly living in accordance with the

divine commandments.
Father Seraphim Rose

For it is a commandment of the LORD not to be silent at a time when the Faith is in jeopardy. Speak, Scripture says, and hold not thy peace.
St. Theodore the Studite

Filled with love, the holy Apostles went into the world, preaching salvation to mankind and fearing nothing, for the Spirit of God was their strength. When St. Andrew was threatened with death upon the cross he did not stay his preaching, he answered: 'If I feared the cross I should not be preaching the Cross." In this manner all the other Apostles, and after them, the martyrs and holy men who wrestled against evil, went forward with joy to meet pain and suffering. For the Holy Spirit, sweet and gracious, draws the soul to love the Lord, and in the sweetness of the Holy Spirit the soul loses her fear of suffering.
St. Silouan the Athonite

Patient endurance kills the despair that kills the soul; it teaches the soul to take comfort and not to grow listless in the face of its many battles and afflictions.
St. Peter of Damascus

Even if the sky were to fall down, even if the earth would rise up, even if the whole world were destroyed, as it is due to do so, today, tomorrow,

don't be concerned with what God is going to do. Let them burn your body, let them fry it, let them take your possessions – don't concern yourself. Give them away – they are not yours. You need your soul and Christ. Even if the whole world were to fall apart, no one can take these two things away from you against your will. Guard these two, and don't lose them.
St. Kosmos Aitolos

Discouragement does not allow the one who falls to get back up, and laziness throws down the one who is upright. The latter deprives us constantly of the goods that we gain; it does not allow us to escape from the evils that are to come. Laziness throws us down even from heaven, while discouragement hurls us down even to the very abyss of wickedness. Indeed, we can quickly return from there if we do not become discouraged.
St. John Chrysostom

Do not reckon as a truly wise man that one whose mind is subject to fear on account of temporal life.
St. Isaac the Syrian

It is better to choose a commendable war than peace which separates from God. The faith which I was taught by the Holy Fathers which I taught at all times without adjusting according to the times, this faith will never stop teaching; I was born with it and I live by it.

St. Gregory the Theologian

Let us be convinced that nothing can happen to us apart from the providence of God.
St. Dorotheos of Gaza

Let us not then be ashamed to confess the Crucified. Be the Cross our seal made with boldness by our fingers on our brow, and on everything; over the bread we eat, and the cups we drink; in our comings in, and goings out; before our sleep, when we lie down and when we rise up; when we are in the way, and when we are still. Great is that preservative; it is without price, for the sake of the poor; without toil, for the sick; since also its grace is from God. It is the Sign of the faithful, and the dread of devils: for He 'triumphed over them in it, having made a show of them openly' [Colossians 2:15]; for when they see the Cross they are reminded of the Crucified; they are afraid of Him, who bruised the heads of the dragon. Despise not the Seal, because of the freeness of the gift; but for this then rather honour your Benefactor.
St. Cyril of Jerusalem

Do not do anything without signing yourself with the sign of the Cross! When you depart on a journey, when you begin your work, when you go to study, when you are alone, and when you are with other people, seal yourself with the Holy Cross on your forehead, your body, your chest, your heart, your lips,

your eyes, your ears. All of you should be sealed with the sign of Christ's victory over hell. Then you will no longer be afraid of charms, evil spirits, or sorcery because these are dissolved by the power of the Cross like wax before fire and like dust before the wind.
Elder Cleopa of Romania

The Judgement

Do not be self-confident until you hear the final sentence passed upon yourself, bearing in mind the guest who got as far as joining in the marriage feast, and then was bound hand and foot and cast out into outer darkness.
St. John Climacus

A person who accepts the revelation of God came in the flesh and then does not live according to it – he is much worse off than any pagan priest or the like.
Father Seraphim Rose

Refuse to listen to the devil when he whispers to you: give me now, and you will give tomorrow to God. No, no! Spend all the hours of your life in a way pleasing to God; keep in your mind the thought that after the present hour you will not be given another and that you will have to render a strict account for every minute of this present hour.
St. Theophon the Recluse

At the Judgment you will not be asked why you did not gain ten talents if you had only one, and you will not even be asked why you gained only one talent on your one, but you will be told that you gained a talent half a talent or a tenth of its worth.

And the reward will not be because you received the talents, but because you gained.

There will be nothing with which to justify yourself— not with nobleness, nor poverty, nor lack of education. When this is not given, there will be no question about it.

But you had hands and feet. You will be asked, what did you gain with them?

You had a tongue, what did you gain with it?

In this way will the inequalities of earthly states be levelled out at God's judgment.

St. Theophan the Recluse

No matter how absurd the idea of the toll houses may seem to our 'wise men,' they will not escape passing through them.

St. Theophan the Recluse

When we receive children from the nurse, let us not accustom them to old wives' stories, but let them learn from their first youth that there is a Judgment, that there is a punishment; let it be infixed in their minds. This fear being rooted in them produces great good effects. For a soul that that has learnt from its first youth to be subdued by this expectation, will not soon shake off this fear. But like a horse obedient to the bridle, having the thought of hell seated upon it walking orderly, it will both speak and utter things

profitable; and neither youth nor riches, not an orphan state, not any other thing, will be able to injure it, having its reason so firm and able to hold out against everything.
St. John Chrysostom

In the case of all who have passed from this world lacking a virtuous life and having had no faith, be an advocate for them, Lord, for the sake of the body which you took from them, so that from the single united body of the world we may offer up praise to Father, Son, and Holy Spirit in the kingdom of heaven, an unending source of eternal life.
St. Isaac the Syrian

Keep careful watch, to ensure that the enemy does not make off with any who are off guard or remiss; and that no heretic may pervert part of what you have been given. Accepting the faith is like putting into the bank the money we have given you; God will ask you for an account of this deposit.
St. Cyril of Jerusalem

If we do the will of Christ we shall obtain rest; but if we neglect His commandments, nothing will rescue us from eternal punishment.
St. Clement of Rome

Too late will they believe in eternal punishment, those who would not believe in eternal life.

St. Cyprian of Carthage

Hope

Remember that God, during your prayers, is watching for your affirmative answer to the question He is asking you: "Do you believe I am able to do this?" To which, from the depths of your heart, you must reply "Yes Lord."
St. John of Krondstadt

Patience, the winter of afflictions will pass, and the beautiful spring will bring the fragrance of the grace of God.
Elder Ephraim of Arizona and Mount Athos

No matter how sinful a Christian has been, he has something precious; faith in the Lord Jesus – and by this faith he will be saved. You too will be saved, only hold fast to Christ, cry out to Him, and He will hear you. Of course, don't cry out with your voice, but with your heart, "Lord Jesus Christ, Son of God, have mercy on me a sinner." And He will have mercy. He will have mercy.
Elder Barsanuphius of Optina

Experience of the Lord's gifts engenders hope; he

who is without experience remains in doubt.
St. John Climacus

For those dead who are unworthy of salvation, God
moves none to pray for them: neither parents, nor
wife, nor husband, nor relatives, nor friends.
St. John of Damascus

Cheerfulness is not a sin. It drives away weariness,
and it is from weariness that despondency comes,
and there is nothing worse than that. It brings with it
everything negative.
St. Seraphim of Sarov

A believer is not one who thinks that God can do
everything, but one who believes that he will obtain
all things. Faith paves the way for what seems
impossible.
St. John Climacus

Only really great faith does not fear ridicule, or shrink
from failure; it does not even think of ridicule and
failure, as it does not doubt success.
Bishop Nikolai Velimirovich

Can you place your hope in the world? Whom has it
not deceived? To whom has it not lied? It promises
much, but gives very little. Only those who hope in
the Lord, according to the words of the Prophet
David, do not sin, i.e., they are not deceived in their

hope!
St. Anthony of Optina

Beware of the spirit of despondency, for it gives birth to every evil. A thousand temptations come from it: agitation, rage, blame, complaint against one's fate, profligate thoughts, constant change of place. The soul then avoids people, believing them to be the cause of its trouble, and does not understand that the cause of the illness is within itself.
St. Seraphim of Sarov

Whoever says that it is impossible to be saved with a wife and children is a deceiver. Abraham had a wife and children and three hundred and eighteen servants, and also much gold and silver, and he was called the friend of God! Many servants of the Church have been saved, and many lovers of the desert; many aristocrats, and many soldiers; many craftsmen, and many farm labourers. Be devout towards God and loving towards men, and you will be saved.
St. Niphon

I have consciousness of my sinfulness, but I live with hope. It is bad to despair, because someone who despairs becomes embittered and loses his willingness and strength. Someone who has hope, on the contrary, advances forward.
St. Porphyrios

What I see around me would drive me insane if I did not know that no matter what happens, God will have the last word.
St. Paisios of Mount Athos

If He was not flesh, whom did the Apostles and Angels see being taken up into heaven? And if He was not God, to Whom was heaven opened, whom did the Powers worship in fear and whom did the Father invite to "Sit at my right hand". As David said, "The Lord said to my Lord, sit at my right hand, etc." If He was not God and man, our salvation is a lie, and the words of the Prophets are lies. But the Prophets spoke the truth, and their testimonies were not lies. The Holy Spirit spoke through them what they had been commanded.
St. Ephraim the Syrian

Only if it is one and the same Christ who is consubstantial with the Father and with men can He save us, for the meeting ground between God and man is Flesh and Christ.
St. Cyril of Alexandria

Do not say, 'This happened by chance, while this came to be of itself.' In all that exists there is nothing disorderly, nothing indefinite, nothing without purpose, nothing by chance ... How many hairs are on your head? God will not forget one of them. Do you see how nothing, even the smallest thing, escapes the

gaze of God?
St Basil the Great

You need not be despondent. Let those be despondent who do not believe in God. For them sorrow is burdensome, of course, because besides earthly enjoyment they have nothing. But believers must not be despondent, for through sorrows they receive the right of sonship, without which it is impossible to enter the Kingdom of Heaven.
St. Barsanuphius of Optina

Humility

An angel fell from Heaven without any other passion except pride, and so we may ask whether it is possible to ascend to Heaven by humility alone, without any other of the virtues.
St. John Climacus

The way of humility is this: self-control, prayer, and thinking yourself inferior to all creatures.
Abba Thithoes

A brother asked "In what manner doth a man come to humility?"
The old man said "In my opinion a man doeth this by restraining and withdrawing himself from everything, and by devoting himself to the labour of the body, and as far as he hath power so to do he should remember his departure from the body, and the awful judgement of God.
Abba Chronius

How rich is the reward bestowed on the person who has come to know his own weakness.
St. Kallistos

A life lived in humility and with an irreproachable conscience brings peace, tranquillity, and true happiness. But wealth, honour, glory and exalted position often serve as the cause of a multitude of sins, and such happiness is not one on which to rely.
St. Makary of Optina

In order to acquire true humility in Christ, one must first bear the humiliation of Christ, one must be the last among his brothers and a servant to them, in order to be a true disciple of Jesus.
Elder Basilisk

Humility is manifested not by him who belittles himself by words, but by him who, having been reviled by someone, does not diminish his love for him.
Blessed Gabriel Dionysiatis of Mount Athos

Before all the virtues is humility, just as before all the passions is gluttony and the desire for worldly things.
Blessed Gabriel Dionysiatis of Mount Athos

When you perceive in yourself something worthy of praise, and you feel a desire to tell others about it, try immediately to destroy this desire with the thought that you will not receive any benefit from relating it, but only harm.
Metropolitan Gregory (Postnikov) of St. Petersburg

Spiritual pride manifests itself by the fact that a proud man dares to make himself a judge of religion and of the Church, and says: "I do not believe in this, and I do not acknowledge this; this I find superfluous, that unnecessary, and this strange or absurd."
St. John of Kronstadt

The Lord sometimes allows people who are devoted to Him to fall into such dreadful vices; and this is in order to prevent them from falling into a still greater sin–pride.
Your temptation will pass and you will spend the remaining days of your life in humility. Only do not forget your sin.
St. Seraphim of Sarov

If God will grant you to do something good, then watch out that you do not attribute it to yourself.
Elder Athanasius of Ploschansk

Humble yourself in everything: only to the humble does the Lord give grace.
Elder Athansius of Ploschansk

I lie down in my sins, and I rise up in my sins.
Abba Sisoes of Pataro

The man who endures accusations against himself with humility has arrived at perfection. He is marvelled at by the holy angels, for there is no other

virtue so great and so hard to achieve.
St Isaac of Syria

What salt is for any food, humility is for every virtue. To acquire it, a man must always think of himself with contrition, self-belittlement and painful self-judgment. But if we acquire it, it will make us sons of God.
St. Isaac the Syrian

A humble man is never rash, hasty or perturbed, never has any hot and volatile thoughts, but at all times remains calm. Even if heaven were to fall and cleave to the earth, the humble man would not be dismayed. Not every quiet man is humble, but every humble man is quiet. There is no humble man who is not self-constrained; but you will find many who are self-constrained without being humble. This is also what the meek humble Lord meant when He said, 'Learn of Me, for I am meek and humble of heart, and ye shall find rest unto your souls.' [Matt 11:29] For the humble man is always at rest, because there is nothing which can agitate or shake his mind. Just as no one can frighten a mountain, so the mind of a humble man cannot be frightened. If it be permissible and not incongruous, I should say that the humble man is not of this world. For he is not troubled and altered by sorrows, nor amazed and enthused by joys, but all his gladness and his real rejoicing are in the things of his Master. Humility is accompanied by

modesty and self-collectedness: that is, chastity of the senses; a moderate voice; mean speech; self-belittlement; poor raiment; a gait that is not pompous; a gaze directed towards the earth; superabundant mercy; easily flowing tears; a solitary soul; a contrite heart; imperturbability to anger; undistributed senses; few possessions; moderation in every need; endurance; patience; fearlessness; manliness of heart born of a hatred of this temporal life; patient endurance of trials; deliberations that are ponderous, not light, extinction of thoughts; guarding of the mysteries of chastity; modesty, reverence; and above all, continually to be still and always to claim ignorance.
St. Isaac the Syrian

Accustom your tongue to say "forgive me", and humility will come to you.
Blessed Gabriel Dionysiatis of Mount Athos

Unhappy is the man whose reputation is greater than his work.
Abba Silvanus

He who is honoured and praised beyond his merits will suffer much condemnation, but he who is held a of no account among men will receive glory i heaven. When you have done all that is commande of you, say "We are unworthy servants; we have onl done what was our duty." (Luke 17 v 10).

The monk should wear a garment of such a kind that he could throw it out of his cell and no one would steal it from him for three days.
Sayings of the Desert Fathers

One day, while St. Anthony was sitting with a certain Abba, a virgin came up and said to the Elder: "Abba, I fast six days of the week and I repeat by heart portions of the Old and New Testament daily." To which the Elder replied: "Does poverty mean the same to you as abundance?" "No", she answered. "Or dishonour the same as praise?" "No, Abba." "Are your enemies the same for you as your friends?" "No", she replied. At that the wise Elder said to her: "Go, get to work, you have accomplished nothing."
St. Peter of Damascus

In our time we see that if a person prays a little more than is customary, reads a little of the Psalter, keeps the fast—he already thinks of himself as better than others, he judges his neighbours, and begins to teach without being asked. All this shows his spiritual emptiness, his departure from the Lord. Fear a high opinion of yourself.
Abbot Nikon Vorobiev

Previously, I wanted everything to go my way, but seeing that nothing was done as I wanted, I began to wish that everything be done as it is done; so it was that everything started to be done as I wanted.

Elder Joseph of Optina

If I still wanted to be popular I would not be the servant of Christ.
St. Gregory Palamas

Fear not hatred from others, but hatred within yourself.
Father Seraphim Rose

When we are young or even middle-aged we can hide our true self. An old person cannot do this. Often the revelation of a person's true self is appalling.
Elder Michael of Valaam

In each matter about which a man boasts himself, God permits that he change, so that he should be humbled, and learn humility.
St. Isaac the Syrian

Every Christian has the power to heal infirmities—not of others, but his own, and not of the body, but of the soul—that is, sins and sinful habits—and to cast out devils, rejecting evil thoughts sown by them, and extinguishing the excitement of passions enflamed by them.
Do this and you will be an apostle, a fulfiller of what the Lord chose you for, an accomplisher of your calling as messenger. When at first you succeed in all this, then perhaps the Lord will appoint you as a

special ambassador—to save others after you have saved yourself; and to help those who are tempted, after you yourself pass through all temptations, and through all experiences in good and evil.

But your job is to work upon yourself: for this you are chosen; the rest is in the hands of God. He who humbles himself shall be exalted.

St. Theophan the Recluse

Humility can be achieved only through faith, fear of God, gentleness and the shedding of all possessions.

It is by means of these that we attain perfect love, through the grace and compassion of our Lord Jesus Christ, to whom be glory through all the ages. Amen.

St. John Cassian

A brother settled outside his village and did not return there for many years. He said to his brethren, "See how many years it is since went back to the village, while you often go up there."

This was told to Abba Poemen who said "I used to go back up there at night and walk all around my village, so that the thought of not having gone up there would not cause me vain-glory."

Sayings of the Desert Fathers

Humility is the only thing we need; one can still fall having virtues other than humility - but with humility one does not fall.

Elder Herman of Mount Athos

Vainglory, like a moth, eats away all our good deeds, and therefore it is better to do all our good deeds in secret so that we do not lose the reward from our Father Who is in heaven.
Archbishop Averky (Taushev)

Consider yourself worse and more infirm than all others in spiritual respects, and despise, hate yourself for your sins, — this is pious and right— and be indulgent to others, respect and love them in spite of their sins.
St. John of Kronstadt

Say to yourself, "It is not me that they slander, but my evil passions; not me that they strike, but that viper which nestles in my heart, and smarts when anybody speaks ill of it. I will comfort myself with the thought that, perhaps, these good people will drive it from my heart by their caustic words, and my heart will then cease to ache."
St. John of Kronstadt

Strive never to offend anyone. Never grow angry. Never teach. When something happens against your will, say: "Glory to God! Glory to God!" One needs to restrain oneself.
Seraphim (Sobolev) of Bogucharsk

God in His goodness has arranged things perfectly, s

that with our gifts, we can help each other, and with our faults, we can be humbled by each other. For every person has some gifts; but everyone also has some faults which one must struggle to overcome.
St. Paisios of Mount Athos

Humility restrains the heart.
St. Isaac the Syrian

A monk also asked Sisoes: How can I attain humility? The saint replied: When someone learns to acknowledge every man as being better than himself, then he has attained humility.
St. Sisoes the Great

Even if we cannot endure much labour because we are weak let us be set on humbling ourselves.
St. Dorotheos of Gaza

He whose will and desire in conversation is to establish his own opinion, even though what he says is true, should recognize that he is sick with the devil's disease.
St. John Climacus

Acts of charity, almsgiving and all the external good works do not suppress the arrogance of the heart; but noetic meditation, the labour of repentance, contrition and humility — these humble the proud mind.

Elder Joseph the Hesychast
When pride retreats from a man, humility begins to dwell in him, and the more pride is diminished, so much more does humility grow. The one gives way to the other as to its opposite. Darkness departs and light appears. Pride is darkness, but humility is light.
St. Tikhon of Zadonsk

When our praisers, or rather our seducers, begin to praise us, let us briefly call to mind the multitude of our sins, and we shall find ourselves unworthy of what is said or done in our honour.
St. John Climacus

Pride

What is sin able to do where repentance is found? And what will love profit where there is pride?
Abba Elijah

He who in his heart is proud of his tears, and secretly condemns those who do not weep, is like a man who asks the king for a weapon against his enemy, and commits suicide with it.
St. John Climacus

For the Lord, a humble sinner is more pleasing than a righteous man who is proud.
Elder Barsanuphius of Optina

A blind person who undertakes to guide others is a deceiver plunging into the pit of destruction those who follow him. As the Lord said: 'if the blind lead the blind, both will fall into the pit' (Matt. 25:14).
St. Symeon the New Theologian

Avoid making idols either of things or of practices.
St. Macarius of Optina

The desire to rule is the mother of heresies.
St. John Chrysostom

The vice of self-esteem, however, is difficult to fight against, because it has many forms and appears in all our activities – in our way of speaking, in what we say and in our silences, at work, in vigils and fasts, in prayer and reading, in stillness and long-suffering. Through all these it seeks to strike down the soldier of Christ.

When it cannot seduce a man with extravagant clothes, it tries to tempt him by means of shabby ones. When it cannot flatter him with honour, it inflates him by causing him to endure what seems to be dishonour. When it cannot persuade him to feel proud of his display of eloquence, it entices him through silence into thinking he has achieved stillness. When it cannot puff him up with the thought of his luxurious table, it lures him into fasting for the sake of praise.

In short, every task, every activity, gives this malicious demon a chance for battle.
St. John Cassian

People of high spirit bear offence nobly and gladly but only the holy and righteous can pass through praise without harm.
St. John Climacus

Wherever God is - there is peace. And the opposite i.

self-evident: where there is envy, enmity, impatience, self-love - there is the devil. Wherever the devil is - there, everything is ruinous, proud and hostile.
St. Anatoly of Optina

Judging Others

Be attentive that you do not judge any soul: for God permits the one who judges his neighbour to fall, so that he may learn sympathy for his weak brother.
Elder Ephraim of Arizona

The Pharisee did not go to the Temple with a healthy soul to boast of his health, but as a man seriously ill with unrighteousness who, in the delirium of his sickness, no longer knows he is ill.
St. Nikolai Velimirovich

We have such a law: If you forgive, it means that God has forgiven you; but if you do not forgive your brother, it means that your sin remains with you.
St. Silouan the Athonite

We see people sinning but we do not see them repenting.
St. John Climacus

Remember that the Lord is in every Christian. When your neighbour comes to you, always have great respect for him, because the Lord is in him, and often expresses His will through him.

St. John of Kronstadt

Never confuse the person formed in the image of God, with the evil that is in him; because evil is but a chance misfortune, an illness, a devilish reverie. But the very essence of the person is the image of God, and this remains in him despite every disfigurement.
St. John of Kronstadt

Even in conversations, we must be careful, because sometimes they begin as spiritual conversations and end up as gossip. And it is not only that we are wasting our time; we are also wasting our souls when condemning someone else, for we have no right to judge other people or other situations.
St. Paisios of Mount Athos

Most importantly, preserve peace with your close ones, insofar as this depends on you. Consider that all sorts of sick people have gathered there in a group; this is so. For this reason you must relate to everyone as they do in a hospital. They don't berate people there (i.e. in a hospital) for having an ailing lung or heart or stomach; they don't say: "O you good-for-nothing blind woman, what's the matter with you that your eyes are infected?"! So, too, you mustn't rail at each other about your spiritual illnesses.
Abbot Nikon Vorobiev

By the purity of our thoughts we can see everyone as

holy and good. When we see them as fools, this comes from our frame of mind.
St. Macarius of Optina

You cannot be too gentle, too kind. Shun even to appear harsh in your treatment of each other. Joy, radiant joy, streams from the face of one who gives and kindles joy in the heart of one who receives. All condemnation is from the devil. Never condemn each other, not even those whom you catch committing an evil deed. We condemn others only because we shun knowing ourselves. When we gaze at our own failings, we see such a morass of filth that nothing in another can equal it. That is why we turn away, and make much of the faults of others. Keep away from the spilling of speech. Instead of condemning others, strive to reach inner peace. Keep silent, refrain from judgement. This will raise you above the deadly arrows of slander, insult, outrage, and will shield your glowing hearts against the evil that creeps around.
St. Seraphim of Sarov

I constantly think of those who lived a wretched life and are now struggling; I love and cherish them more than those who do not suffer from passions. Even a shepherd will be more compassionate with the injured or sickly sheep and will give it more attentive care until it gets back on its feet again.
St. Paisios of Mount Athos

If we are scandalized, the evil is within us not outside

When you feel scandalized, you should ask yourself, How many do I scandalize? In God's name, shouldn't I tolerate my brother or sister? How does God tolerate me with all the things I do?
St. Paisios of Mount Athos

If you see a man who has sinned and you do not pity him, the grace of God will leave you. Whoever curses bad people, and does not pray for them, will never come to know the grace of God.
St. Silouan the Athonite

A discerning man, when he eats grapes, takes only the ripe ones and leaves the sour. Thus also the discerning mind carefully marks the virtues which he sees in any person. A mindless man seeks out the vices and failings ... Even if you see someone sin with your own eyes, do not judge; for often even your eyes are deceived.
St. John Climacus

Fire and water are incompatible; and so is judging others in one who wants to repent. If you see someone falling into sin at the very moment of his death, even then do not judge him, because the Divine judgment is hidden from men. Some have fallen openly into great sins, but they have done greater good deeds in secret; so their critics were tricked, getting smoke instead of the sun.
St. John Climacus

He who busies himself with the sins of others, or judges his brother on suspicion, has not yet even begun to repent or to examine himself so as to discover his own sins.
St. Maximos the Confessor

Do we refuse to forgive? God, too, will refuse to forgive us. As we treat our neighbours, so also does God treat us. The forgiveness or unforgiveness of your sins, then, and hence also your salvation or destruction, depend on you yourself. For without forgiveness of sins there is no salvation. You can see for yourself how serious it is.
St. Tikhon of Zadonsk

Your own malice is the bitterest of all evils. Is it then possible to correct malice by means of evil? Having a beam in your own eye, can you pull out the mote from the eye of another?
Evil and faults are corrected by good, by love, kindness, meekness, humility, and patience.
St. John of Kronstadt

Every man on earth is sick with the fever of sin, with the blindness of sin and is overcome with its fury. As sins consist mostly of malice and pride, it is necessary to treat everyone who suffers from the malady of sin with kindness and love. This is an important truth which we often forget. Very often we act in the

opposite manner: we add malice to malice by our anger, we oppose pride with pride. Thus, evil grows within us and does not decrease; it is not cured – rather it spreads.
St. John of Kronstadt

Since the enemy watches you constantly, waiting for an opportunity to sow evil in you, be doubly watchful over yourself, lest you fall in the nets spread for you. As soon as he shows you some fault in your neighbour, hasten to repel this thought, lest it take root in you and grow. Cast it out, so that no trace is left in you, and replace it by the thought of the good qualities you know your neighbour to possess, or of those people generally should have. If you still feel the impulse to pass judgment, add to this the truth that you are given no authority for this and that the moment you assume this authority you thereby make yourself worthy of judgment and condemnation, not before powerless men, but before God, the all-powerful Judge of all. This reversal of thoughts is the strongest means, not only for repelling accidental critical thoughts, but also for completely freeing yourself of this vice.
St. Theophan the Recluse

The man who cries out against evil men but does not pray for them will never know the grace of God.
St. Silouan the Athonite

You receive the Cup which seemingly comes from the hands of man. What is it to you whether the bearer of the Cup acts righteously or unrighteously? As a follower of Jesus, your concern is to act righteously; to receive the Cup with thanksgiving to God and with a living faith; and courageously to drink it to the dregs.
St. Ignatius Brianchaninov

Who hated sin more than the saints? But they did not hate the sinners at the same time, nor condemn them, nor turn away from them. But they suffered with them, admonished them, comforted them, gave them remedies as sickly members, and did all they could to heal them.
St. Dorotheos of Gaza

If you see your neighbour in sin, don't look only at this, but also think about what he has done or does that is good, and infrequently trying this in general while not partially judging, you will find that he is better than you.
St. Basil the Great

Humble yourself before everyone and consider yourself the worst of all. If we have not committed the sins that others have, perhaps this is because we did not have the opportunity – the situation and circumstances were different. In each person there is something good and something bad; we usually see

only the vices in people and we see nothing that is good.
St. Ambrose of Optina

Anger

The beginning of freedom from anger is silence of the lips when the heart is agitated; the middle is silence of the thoughts when there is disturbance in the soul; and the end is an imperturbable calm under the breath of unclean winds.
St. John Climacus

Wrath is a reminder of hidden hatred.
St John Climacus

As with the appearance of light, darkness retreats; so at the fragrance of humility, all anger and bitterness vanishes.
St. John Climacus

Someone who bears a grudge while he prays is like a person who sows in the sea and expects to reap a harvest.
St. Isaac the Syrian

Do not pass through the streets of the hot-tempered and quarrelsome, lest your heart be filled with anger and the darkness of delusion dominate your soul.

St. Isaac the Syrian

Flee from all evil and anything resembling it. Do not get angry, for anger leads to murder. Do not get into passionate tempers or be quarrelsome or boil with rage, for all these things breed murder.
The Didache

The Lord dwells in those who have patience, but the devil dwells in anger.
Hermas of Rome

God placed the faculty of anger within us so that we can direct this feeling toward our own sins, the passions and the devil.
Metropolitan Anthony Khrapovitsky

Some are most careful about the food they take in but negligent about the words they give out. Such men do not know how to remove anger from the heart or lust from the flesh. Only through the removal of these things is a pure heart established within us by the renewing Spirit.
Ilias the Presbyter

Dispassion does not mean that a man feels no passions, but that he does not accept any of them.
St. Isaac the Syrian

He who says that he loves the Lord but is angry with his brother is like a man that dreams he is running.
St. John Climacus

Remembrance of wrongs is the consummation of anger, the keeper of sins, hatred of righteousness, ruin of virtues, poison of the soul, worm of the mind, shame of prayer, stopping of supplication, estrangement of love, a nail stuck in the soul, pleasureless feeling beloved in the sweetness of bitterness, continuous sin, unsleeping transgression, hourly malice. This dark and hateful passion, I mean remembrance of wrongs, is one of those that are produced but have no offspring. That is why we do not intend to say much about it.
He who has put a stop to anger has also destroyed remembrance of wrongs; because childbirth continues only while the father is alive.
St. John Climacus

If the Holy Spirit is peace of soul, as He is said to be, and as He is in reality, and if anger is disturbance of heart, as it actually is and as it is said to be, then nothing so prevents His presence in us as anger.
St. John Climacus

No matter what provokes it, anger blinds the soul's eyes, preventing it from seeing the Sun of Righteousness.
St. John Cassian

What is the use of sparing fowl and fishes if we eat our own brothers?
St. John Chrysostom

Love

Faith and love are inseparable between them and one relates to the other, and confirms one another and defines each other, and wherever one is absent the other is also absent from there and wherever one is found the other is found there too. Amen.
Elder Arsenios Galanopoulos, the Cave-dweller

Have the heart of a son toward God, the mind of a judge toward yourself, and toward your neighbour the heart of a mother.
St. Cleopas of Romania

If you find there is no love in you but you want to have it, then do works of love, although they may have been begun without love. The Lord will see your desire and attempt, and will put love into your heart.
St. Ambrose of Optina

Love will not come of itself without our zeal, effort and activity.
St. John of Kronstadt

Fight against every worldly enticement, against every material enticement that hinders you from fulfilling

Christ's commandments, love God with all your heart, and care with all your strength for the salvation of your own soul, and the souls of others, be soul-loving.
St. John of Kronstadt

The fear of hell trains beginners to flee from evil; the desire for the reward of good things given to the advanced and eagerness for the practice of virtues. But the mystery of love removes the mind from all created things, causing it to be blind to all that is less than God. Only those who have become blind to all that is less than God does the Lord instruct by showing them more divine things.
St. Maximus the Confessor

As the memory of fire does not warm the body, so faith without love does not bring about the illumination of knowledge in the soul.
St. Maximus the Confessor

The person who loves God cannot help loving every man as himself, even though he is grieved by the passions of those who are not yet purified. But when they amend their lives, his delight is indescribable and knows no bounds.
St. Maximos the Confessor

Obedience is love, but disobedience is non-love, it is the trampling upon love. Never decline from obedience.

Archbishop Seraphim (Sobolev) of Bogucharsk

A man who is wrathful with us is a sick man; we must apply a plaster to his heart - love; we must treat him kindly, speak to him gently, lovingly. And if there is not deeply-rooted malice against us within him, but only a temporary fit of anger, you will see how his heart, or his malice, will melt away through your kindness and love - how good will conquer evil. A Christian must always be kind, gracious, and wise in order to conquer evil by good.
St. John of Kronstadt

Love is essentially the banishment of every kind of contrary thought, for love thinketh no evil.
St. John Climacus

Love is greater than prayer, because prayer is a particular virtue but love embraces all virtues.
St. John Climacus

Even a mother does not so cling to the babe at her breast as a son of love clings to the Lord at all times.
St. John Climacus

Let mercy outweigh all else in you. Let our compassion be a mirror where we may see in ourselves that likeness and that true image which belong to the Divine nature and Divine essence. A heart hard and unmerciful will never be pure.

St. Isaac the Syrian

Conquer men by your gentle kindness, and make zealous men wonder at your goodness. Put the lover of justice to shame by your compassion. With the afflicted be afflicted in mind. Love all men, but keep distant from all men.

St. Isaac the Syrian

Be extremely careful not to offend anyone in word or deed, for it is a grave sin. When someone is offended, God, Who loves the man, is also offended, for there can be no offending man without offending God.

St. Tikhon of Zadonsk

One who performs saving works simply from the fear of hell follows the way of bondage, and he who does the same just in order to be rewarded with the Kingdom of Heaven follows the path of a bargainer with God. The one they call a slave, the other a hireling. But God wants us to come to Him as sons to their Father, He wants us to behave honourably from love of Him and zeal for His service, He wants us to find our happiness in uniting ourselves with Him in a saving union of mind and heart.

From *The Way Of A Pilgrim*

If parents do not pursue a life of holiness and if they don't engage in spiritual struggle, they make great mistakes and transmit the faults they have within

them. If the parents do not live a holy life and do not display love towards each other, the devil torments the parents with the reactions of the children. Love, harmony and understanding between parents are what are required for the children. This provides a great sense of security and certainty.
St. Porphyrios

Whoever prays for those who hurt him lays the demons low; but he who opposes his affronter is bound to the demons.
St. Mark the Ascetic

There is no greater love than that a man lays down his life for his neighbour. When you hear someone complaining and you struggle with yourself and do not answer him back with complaints; when you are hurt and bear it patiently, not looking for revenge; then you are laying down your life for your neighbour.
Abba Poemen

One cannot love God if one has unkind feelings for even a single human being.
Abbot Nikon Vorobiev

Don't wage your Christian struggle with sermons and arguments, but with true love. When we argue, others react. When we love people, they are moved and we win them over. When we love we think that we offe

something to others, but in reality we are the first to benefit.
St. Porphyrios

Whoever will not love his enemies cannot know the Lord and the sweetness of the Holy Spirit. The Holy Spirit teaches us to love our enemies in such way that we pity their souls as if they were our own children.
St. Silouan the Athonite

Holy Relics are the earthly remains of those who have been taught by none other than Christ Himself to love their enemies even unto death, the death of the Cross, which is His glory, and which by grace becomes their glory too. Love for enemies is not a moral injunction, it is the fundamental criterion for the Christian way of life. This is Salvation.
St. Silouan the Athonite

Christ prayed for those that crucified Him: 'Father, count not this sin against them; they know not what they do.' Archdeacon Stephen prayed for those who stoned him so that the Lord would not judge this sin against them. And so we, if we wish to retain grace, must pray for our enemies. If you do not find pity on a sinner who will suffer in flames, then you do not carry the grace of the Holy Spirit, but rather an evil spirit; and while you yet live, you must free yourself from his clutches through repentance.
St. Silouan the Athonite

Love overcomes all obstacles; for it, everything difficult is easy, everything unpleasant is pleasant, and everything heavy is light.
Metropolitan Gregory (Postnikov) of St. Petersburg

It is madness for a Christian to be envious. In Christ we have all received infinitely great blessings.
St. John of Kronstadt

In order to test yourself, whether you love your neighbour in accordance with the Gospel, pay attention to yourself at the time when others offend you... If you remain calm on such occasions, are not filled with the spirit of enmity, hatred, impatience — if you continue to love these persons as much as previously, before their offences or negligence, then you do love your neighbour in accordance with the Gospel.
St. John of Kronstadt

Fasts and vigils, the study of Scripture, renouncing possessions and everything worldly are not in themselves perfection, as we have said; they are it tools. For perfection is not to be found in them; it i acquired through them. It is useless, therefore, t boast of our fasting, vigils, poverty, and reading c Scripture when we have not achieved the love of Go and our fellow men. Whoever has achieved love ha God within himself and his intellect is always wit

God.
St. John Cassian

True, unselfish, pure love for God and man is impossible except under the action of faith in the divinity of Christ the Saviour—faith in the fact that He is the Incarnate Son of God who came down to earth to save mankind.
Archbishop Averky (Taushev)

When we approach someone with pain and true love, then this true love of Christ transforms our neighbour.
St. Paisios of Mount Athos

A dog is better than I am, for he has love and he does not judge.
Abba Xanthios

"But I say to you," the Lord says, "love your enemies, do good to those who hate you, pray for those who persecute you." Why did He command these things? So that He might free you from hatred, sadness, anger and grudges, and might grant you the greatest possession of all, perfect love, which is impossible to possess except by the one who loves all equally in imitation of God.
St. Maximus the Confessor

If we want, Christian, to have our heart filled with

divine love we must first empty them of the love of this world, its frivolous and sinful customs and then turn our hearts to the one God, our only good and happiness and eternal beatitude.

St. Tikhon of Zadonsk

"Love covers a multitude of sins," (I Pet. 4:8). That is, for love towards one's neighbour, God forgives the sins of the one who loves.

St. Theophan the Recluse

When a man really considers his neighbour as himself, he will never tolerate having more than his neighbour. If he does have more, but refuses to share things generously until he himself becomes as poor as his neighbour, then he will find that he has not fulfilled the commandment of the master. He no longer wants to give to all who ask, and instead turns away from someone who asks of him while she still has a penny or a crust of bread. He has not treated his neighbour as he would like to be treated by him. In fact, even if a man had given food and drink and clothes to all the poor, even the least, and had done everything else for them, he has only to despise or neglect a single one and it will be reckoned as if he had passed by Christ and God and He was hungry and thirsty.

St. Symeon the New Theologian

We are commanded to have only one enemy, the

devil. With him never be reconciled! But with a brother, never be at enmity in thy heart.
St. John Chrysostom

Let the mouth also fast from disgraceful speeches and railings. For what does it profit if we abstain from fish and fowl and yet bite and devour our brothers and sisters? The evil speaker eats the flesh of his brother and bites the body of his neighbour.
St. John Chrysostom

The more one is united to his neighbour the more he is united to God.
St. Dorotheos of Gaza

Do not ask for love from your neighbour, for if you ask and he does not respond, you will be troubled. Instead show your love for your neighbour and you will be at rest, and so will bring your neighbour to love.
St. Dorotheos of Gaza

Struggles

Let us walk the straight path of sorrow, that we might become worthy and have God as our protector.
St. Ephraim the Syrian

Work is a blessing, a gift from God. Work gives vigour to the body and refreshes the mind. If God had not given us work, man would have become mouldy. Those who are diligent continue to work into their old age.
St. Paisios of Mount Athos

Let us become imitators of Christ's endurance... for He made this suffering an example for us.
St. Polycarp

Let all the torments of hell come upon me, for I suffer for the love of Christ.
St. Ignatius of Antioch

Do not fear the conflict, do not flee it. Where there is no struggle, there is no virtue; where faith and love are not tempted, it is not possible to be sure whether they are really present. They are proved and revealed in adversity, that is, in difficult and grievous

circumstances, both outward and inward – during sickness, sorrow, and privation.
St. John Kronstadt

When man lives in full liberty, in abundance and prosperity, then he grows in body and does not grow in spirit, does not bring forth fruits— good works; whilst when he lives in straightness, in poverty, sickness, misfortune, and afflictions, in a word, when his animal nature is crushed, then he grows spiritually, bears flowers of virtue, ripens and brings forth rich fruits. This is why the path of those who love God is a narrow one.
St. John of Kronstadt

When you are subjected to the malicious and furious violence of the passions, and to the harassments of the Devil, during the fulfilment of various works for God, accept these sufferings as sufferings for the name of Christ, and rejoice in your sufferings, thanking God; for the Devil is preparing you, without knowing it himself, the most shining crowns from the Lord.
St. John of Kronstadt

He who loses his cross loses his Christianity.
Metropolitan Saba (Esber)

There will come a time when not the persecutions but money and the goods of this world will take people

far from God. Then many more souls will be lost than in the time of the persecutions. On the one hand, they will be putting gold on the domes and will put the crosses on them and, on the other hand, everywhere evil and falsehood will reign. The true Church will always be persecuted. They who want to be saved will be saved with illnesses and afflictions. The way in which the persecutions will occur will be very sly and it will be very difficult for one to foresee the persecutions. Dreadful will be that time; I pity those who will be living then.
St. Seraphim of Viritsa

Maladies in our eyes only appear painful, unpleasant and terrible. It is seldom that any one of us during the time of sickness represents to himself the profit which his illness brings to his soul; but in God's all wise and most merciful Providence, not a single malady remains without some profit to our soul.
St. John of Kronstadt

When sorrow comes to us, we must await consolations, but after the consolation, we must again await sorrows.
St. Hilarion of Optina

Every physical and spiritual task which does not involve pain and toil and trouble never bears fruit for the person who engages in it, for the Kingdom of Heaven is taken by violence and the violent lay hold

of it.
St. Ignatius Brianchaninov

If you are not willing to repent through freely choosing to suffer, unsought sufferings will providentially be imposed on you.
St Thalassios the Libyan

If one loses his cross, his life becomes cold and tepid, without cooperation with God.
Metropolitan Saba (Esber)

There is not, never has been, nor ever will be a place on the earth without sorrows. A place without sorrows can only be in the heart, when the Lord is within it.
St. Nikon of Optina

It is sinful to give up to sadness. We are exiles on earth. Exiles do not wonder at insult and injury. We are under God's penance and a penance consists of deprivations and difficulties. We are ill in soul and body and bitter medicine is useful for the ill.
St. Theophil of the Kiev Caves

A fish that is alive swims against the flow of water. One that is dead floats down with the water. A true Christian goes against the current of a sinful age. A false one is swept away by its swiftness.
St. Philaret of Moscow

No matter what bitterness has befallen you, no matter what unpleasantness has happened to you, say, "I shall endure this for Jesus Christ!" and it will be easier for you. For the name of Jesus Christ is powerful. Through it all unpleasantness is calmed, and demons disappear. Your disappointments will also be calmed and your pusillanimity will be quieted.
St. Anthony of Optina

Temptations are medicines and healing herbs that heal our visible passions and our invisible wounds. So have patience in order to profit every day, to store up wages, rest, and joy in the heavenly kingdom. For the night of death is coming when no one will be able to work anymore. Therefore, hurry. Time is short.
St. Joseph the Hesychast

Let all involuntary suffering teach you to remember God, and you will not lack occasion for repentance.
St. Mark the Ascetic

Do not claim to have acquired virtue unless you have suffered affliction, for without affliction virtue has not been tested.
St. Mark the Ascetic

Until a man's earthly life finishes its course, up to the very departure of the soul from the body, the struggle between sin and righteousness continues within him

However, high a spiritual and moral state one might achieve, a gradual or even headlong and deep fall into the abyss of sin is always possible. Therefore, communion of the holy Body and Blood of Christ, which strengthens our contact with Him and refreshes us with the living streams of the grace of the Holy Spirit flowing through the Body of the Church, is necessary for everyone.

St. John of Shanghai

In proportion to your humility you are given patience in your woes; and in proportion to your patience the burden of your afflictions is made lighter and you will find consolation; in proportion to your consolation, your love of God increases; and in proportion to your love, your joy in the Holy Spirit is magnified. Once men have truly become His sons, our tenderly compassionate Father does not take away their temptations from them when it is His pleasure to 'make for them a way to escape' (1 Cor. 10:13), but instead He gives His sons patience in their trials. All these good things are given into the hand of their patience for the perfecting of their souls.

St. Isaac the Syrian

God, in His very benevolence, often allows misfortunes to befall even the righteous, so that He may, in this way, manifest to others the latent faith hidden in him.

St. John of Damascus

He who endures distress, will be granted joys; and he who bears with unpleasant things, will not be deprived of the pleasant.
St. Nilus of Sinai

Struggle to the very end. The whole point of the struggle is not to be delivered from the struggle, as it will go on forever. The reason to struggle is that the more you do, the better chances you have of being successful in your struggle.
Elder Sergei of Vanves

Sometimes men are tested by pleasure, sometimes by distress or by physical suffering. By means of His prescriptions the Physician of souls administers the remedy according to the cause of the passions lying hidden in the soul.
St. Maximos the Confessor

The Christian who is struggling in the world is helped when he has relationships with spiritual people.
St. Paisios of Mount Athos

Concern for one's soul means hardship and humility for through these God forgives us all our sins.
St. Thalassios the Libyan

A continuously happy life produces extremely unhappy consequences. In nature we see that there are not always pleasant springs and fruitful summers, and sometimes autumn is rainy and winter cold and snowy, and there is flooding and wind and storms, and moreover the crops fail and there are famine, troubles, sicknesses and many other misfortunes. All of this is beneficial so that man might learn through prudence, patience and humility. For the most part, in times of plenty he forgets himself, but in times of various sorrows he becomes more attentive to his salvation.

St. Ambrose of Optina

We must be prepared to accept the will of God. The Lord permits all sorts of things to happen to us contrary to our will, for if we always have it our way, we will not be prepared for the Kingdom of Heaven. Neither heaven nor earth will receive those who are self-willed. God has a Divine plan for each one of us, and we must submit to His plan. We must accept life as it is given to us, without asking, "Why me?" We must know that nothing on earth or in heaven ever happens without the will of God or His permission.

Elder Thaddeus (Strabulovich) of Vitovnica

To have faith in Christ means more than simply despising the delights of this life. It means we should bear all our daily trials that may bring us sorrow, distress, or unhappiness, and bear them patiently for as long as God wishes and until He comes to visit us. For it is said, 'I waited on the Lord and He came to

me.'
St. Symeon the New Theologian

It is through victories in small things that the fathers won their great battles.
St. Peter of Damascus

Keep striving until the fire of heresy is put out, before it consumes the Church.
St. Basil the Great

Someone is tested through the trials of life. It is there that you see if he has real love, a true spirit of sacrifice. And when we say that someone has the spirit of sacrifice, we mean that at the time of danger he does not consider himself but thinks of the others.
St. Paisios of Mount Athos

As wax cannot take the imprint of a seal unless it is warmed or softened thoroughly, so a man cannot receive the seal of God's holiness unless he is tested by labours and weaknesses.
St. Diadochus, bishop of Photike in Epirus

The cross is not merely a sort of beautiful spiritual meditation. It is also enduring suffering in order to stand against the sinful world.
Metropolitan Saba (Esber)

Almost everyone feels more or less uneasy most of their life in this earthly existence. This is a part of the cross that we all must bear.
Elder Sergei of Vanves

I saw that there was no tragedy in God. Tragedy is to be found solely in the fortunes of the man whose gaze has not gone beyond the confines of this earth
St. Sophrony Sakharov

It is difficult for you, but think of how it was for the Saviour on the Cross. The end is near; life passes quickly. We are guests on earth, migratory birds.
Archbishop Seraphim (Sobolev) of Bogucharsk

Where there are no labours, there are stagnation and the extinction of the sparks of life.
St. Theophan the Recluse

Someone who faces every problem spiritually is not exhausted.
Saint Paisios of Mount Athos

Did the Saints have the kind of joy we are seeking today? Did Panagia have such joy? Did Jesus go around laughing? Which Saint has gone through this life without pain? Which Saint had the joy sought by many present-day Christians who do not want to hear anything unpleasant, who do not want to worry or lose their serenity?

Elder Paisios of Mount Athos

Do not fear bodily privations, but fear spiritual privation.
St. John of Kronstadt

When you see your body wasted away through sickness, do not murmur against God, but say, The Lord gave and the Lord has taken away; blessed be the Name of the Lord (Job 1:21). You are accustomed to look upon your body as upon your own inalienable property, but that is quite wrong, because your body is God's edifice.
St. John of Kronstadt

We must acknowledge all such everyday work that is not opposed to moral law and that we must do according to our position, as God's work, as work entrusted to us by the Lord God Himself. We must acknowledge our daily work as such because the Lord God established various sanctioned positions and professions in human society, and it was the Lord God, and not we, Who put us or allows us to be in the positions or professions in which we find ourselves in life.
Metropolitan Gregory (Postnikov) of St. Petersburg

Sweet life is not experienced by those who enjoy it in a worldly way, but rather by those who live spiritually and accept bitterness with joy, like

healing herb for the soul's health, and eat only for their bodily preservation.
Saint Paisios of Mount Athos

If the work that you are doing is prolonged, unpleasant, hard, and is someone else's as well, then to keep your soul in a holy and God-pleasing disposition and to protect yourself from any foolish disposition of soul, support yourself while you work with edifying singing, as long as it is not ruled out by the work itself or the place and time. Edifying singing greatly cheers, softens, and calms the soul. If, as is well known, even unedifying, foolish singing during work greatly cheers a person as he works, so much more will edifying singing.
Metropolitan Gregory (Postnikov) of St. Petersburg

God give us the strength to pursue the path of crucifixion; there is no other way to be Christian.
Father Seraphim Rose

When conversion does take place, the process of revelation occurs in a very simple way; a person is in need, he suffers, and then somehow the other world opens up. The more you are in suffering and difficulties and are desperate for God, the more He is going to come to your aid, reveal Who He is, and show you the way to get out.
Father Seraphim Rose

We have to be aware that what is being pounded in upon us is all of one piece; it has a certain rhythm, a certain message to give us, this message of self-worship, of relaxing, of letting go, of enjoying yourself, of giving up any thought of the other world... It is actually an education in atheism. We have to fight back by knowing just what the world is trying to do to us.
Father Seraphim Rose

To be Christian is to be crucified in this time and in any time since Christ came for the first time. His life is the example and warning to us all. We must be crucified personally, mystically; for through crucifixion is the only path to resurrection; if we would rise with Christ, we must be humbled with him even to the ultimate humiliation, being devoured and spit forth by the uncomprehending world.
Father Seraphim Rose

Why do men learn through pain and suffering, and not through pleasure and happiness? Very simply, because pleasure and happiness accustom one to satisfaction with the things given in this world, whereas pain and suffering drive one to seek a more profound happiness beyond the limitations of this world. I am at this moment in some pain, and I call on the Name of Jesus—not necessarily to relieve the pain, but that Jesus, in Whom alone we may transcend this world, may be with me during it, and His will be done in me. But in pleasure I do not call on Him; I am content then with what I have, and I think I need no more. And why is a philosophy of pleasure untenable?—because pleasure is impermanent and unreliable, and pain is inevitable. In pain and suffering Christ speaks to us, and thus God is kind to give them to us, yes, and evil too—for in all of these we glimpse something of what must lie beyond, if there really exists what our hearts most deeply desire.

Father Seraphim Rose

A human being who does not endure courageously the unpleasant burdens of temptations, will never produce fruit worthy of the divine wine-press and eternal harvest, not even if one possesses all other virtues. For one is only perfected through zealously enduring both all the voluntary and involuntary afflictions.

St. Gregory Palamas

The Most High planted in the middle of Paradise the thrice blessed wood, the gift of life for us, in order that, in approaching it, Adam might find eternal and immortal life, But he did not strive earnestly to know this life, and he failed to attain it, and revealed death. However, the robber, seeing how the plant in Eden had been beautifully transplanted in Golgotha, recognized the life in it and said to himself: `This is what my father lost formerly In Paradise.'

St. Romanos the Melodist

Do not fear sorrows, but fear the stubbornness of heretics who try to separate a man from Christ, which is why Christ commanded us to consider them as pagans and pharisees.
St. Anatoly of Optina

Woe to those who are rich, who are full, who laugh, and who are praised. But good shall come to those who endure every wrongful accusation, beating, robbery, or compulsory difficulty. This is completely opposite to what people usually think and feel! The thoughts of God are as far from human thoughts as heaven is from the earth. How else could it be? We are in exile; and it is not remarkable for those in exile to be offended and insulted. We are under a penance the penance consists of deprivations and labours. We are sick; and most useful for the sick are bitter medicines. The Saviour Himself all of His life did no have a place to lay His head, and He finished His life on the cross - why should His followers have a better lot? The Spirit of Christ is the spirit of preparedness to suffer and bear good-naturedly all that i sorrowful. Comfort, arrogance, splendour, and ease are all foreign to its searching and tastes. Its path lie in the fruitless, dreary desert. The model is the forty year wandering of the Israelites in the desert. Wh follows this path? Everyone who sees Canaan beyon the desert, boiling over with milk and honey. Durin

his wandering he too receives manna, however not from the earth, but from heaven; not bodily, but spiritually. All the glory is within.
St. Theophan the Recluse

Do not try to discover the causes of your trials or where they come from, but only pray to God that you may bear them gratefully.
St. Kallistos

What draws down God's grace upon someone is a heart moved to give thanks unceasingly, while a heart continually inclined to grumble and complain brings the soul into temptation.
St. Isaac the Syrian

The sensible man, taking into account the remedial effect of the divine prescriptions, gladly bears the sufferings which they bring upon him, since he is aware that they have no cause other than his own sin. But when the fool, ignorant of the supreme wisdom of God's providence, sins and is corrected, he regards either God or men as responsible for the hardships he suffers.
St. Maximos the Confessor

God does not forsake you. It is because he wishes to increase your glory that oftentimes he permits you to fall sick. Keep up your courage so that you may also hear him say: 'Do you think I have dealt with you

otherwise than that you may be shown to be just?'
St. John Chrysostom

Troubles are usually the brooms and shovels that smooth the road to a good man's fortune; and many a man curses the rain that falls upon his head, and knows not that it brings abundance to drive away hunger.
St. Basil the Great

Without a struggle and shedding your blood, don't expect freedom from the passions. Our earth produces thorns and thistles after the Fall. We have been ordered to clean it, but only with much pain, bloody hands, and many sighs are the thorns and thistles uprooted. So weep, shed streams of tears, and soften the earth of your heart. Once the ground is wet you can easily uproot the thorns.
St. Joseph the Hesychast

Let all the torments of hell come upon me, for I suffer for the love of Christ.
St. Ignatius of Antioch

If we are not ready to die unto Christ's sufferings, His life is not within us.
St Ignatius of Antioch

Good Works

It goes without saying that good works are essential for success in the spiritual life, for they demonstrate the presence of good will in us, without which there is no moving forward; in turn, good works themselves strengthen, develop, and deepen this good will.
Archbishop Averky (Taushev)

And how can one work for God? You already know: you must pray and be vigilant over yourself, struggle with thoughts, not argue over trifles, humble yourself before others (even if this causes your work to suffer; afterwards you will gain all the more), make peace quickly, reveal your thoughts, partake more often of the Holy Mysteries, and so forth.
Abbot Nikon Vorobiev

Worthless is the charity of the man who bestows it unwillingly, because material charity is not his, but God's gift, whilst only the disposition of the heart belongs to him. This is why many charities prove almost worthless, for they were bestowed unwillingly, grudgingly, without respect for the person of our neighbour.
St. John of Kronstadt

Why did not the Almighty create the world at once, but in six days? In order to teach man, by deeds, to perform his work gradually, not hurriedly, but with consideration.
St John of Kronstadt

Let this always be the aim of your conduct: to be courteous and respectful to all.
Venerable Isaac the Syrian, bishop of Nineveh

It is a good thing to believe in Christ, because without faith in Christ it is impossible for anyone to be saved; but one must also be instructed in the word of truth and understand it. It is a good thing to be instructed in the word of truth, and to understand it is essential; but one must also receive Baptism in the name of the Holy and Life-giving Trinity, for the bringing to life of the soul. It is a good thing to receive Baptism and through it a new spiritual life; but it is necessary that this mystical life, or this mental enlightenment in the spirit, also should be consciously felt. It is a good thing to receive with feeling the mental enlightenment in the spirit; but one must manifest also the works of light. It is a good thing to do the works of light; but one must also be clothed in the humility and meekness of Christ for perfect likeness to Christ. He who attains this and becomes meek and humble of heart, as if these were his natural dispositions, will unfailingly enter into the Kingdom

of Heaven and into the joy of His Lord.
St. Symeon the New Theologian

Seek to distinguish yourself from others only in your generosity. Be like gods to the poor, imitating God's mercy. Humanity has nothing so much in common with God as the ability to do good.
St. Gregory the Theologian

Hatred is the devil's poison, and just as when we put a little yeast in a hundred pounds of flour it has such power that it causes all the dough to rise, so it is with hatred. It transforms all the good we have done into the devil's poison.
St. Kosmas Aitolo

Let it be understood that those who are not found living as He taught are not Christian - even though they profess with the lips the teaching of Christ.
St. Justin Martyr

Those who labour for the vain things in life strive to make those who labour for God's sake stumble, that they might not be confronted with examples that accuse their conscience; but in so doing they only embellish the crowns of conscientious labourers.
St. Ephraim the Syrian

We should never say that nothing is important. On the contrary, everything is important. Even the

smallest of our actions impacts our eternal salvation.
Elder Sergei of Vanves

Fasting, prayer, alms, and every other good Christian deed is good in itself, but the purpose of the Christian life consists not only in the fulfillment of one or another of them. The true purpose of our Christian life is the acquisition of the Holy Spirit of God. But fasting, prayer, alms and every good deed done for the sake of Christ is a means to the attainment of the Holy Spirit. Note that only good deeds done for the sake of Christ bear the fruit of the Holy Spirit. Everything else that is not done for the sake of Christ, even if it is good, does not bring us a reward in the life to come, not does it bring the grace of God in this life. This is why our Lord Jesus Christ said, 'Whoever gathereth not with me scattereth' (Matt. 12:30).
St. Seraphim of Sarov

One must do good deeds but not place hope in them. To place hope in one's deeds is a sign of self-reliance.
Elder Macarius of Optina

Compel yourselves; say the prayer; stop idle talk close your mouths to criticism; place doors and lock against unnecessary words. Time passes and does no come back, and woe to us if time goes by withou spiritual profit.
Elder Ephraim of Mount Athos and Arizona

For virtue is a light and buoyant thing, and all who live in her way "fly like clouds" as Isaiah says, "and as doves with their young ones"; but sin is a heavy affair, as another of the prophets says, "sitting upon a talent of lead".

St. Gregory of Nyssa

He who wants to do something and cannot is, in the eyes of God who sees our hearts, as though he has done it. This should be understood as being so in relation to good and evil alike.

St. Mark the Ascetic

Feeding the hungry is a greater work than raising the dead.

St. John Chrysostom

Let thy mind fast from vain thoughts; let thy memory fast from remembering evil; let thy will fast from evil desire; let thine eyes fast from bad sights: turn away thine eyes that thou mayest not see vanity; let thine ears fast from vile songs and slanderous whispers; let thy tongue fast from slander, condemnation, blasphemy, falsehood, deception, foul language and every idle and rotten word; let thy hands fast from killing and from stealing another's goods; let thy legs fast from going to evil deeds: Turn away from evil, and do good

St. Tikhon of Zadonsk

The aim of all those who live in God is to please our Lord Jesus Christ and become reconciled with God the Father through receiving the Holy Spirit, thus securing their salvation, for in this consists the salvation of every soul. If this aim and this activity is lacking, all other labour is useless and all other striving is in vain. Every path of life which does not lead to this is without profit.

St. Symeon the New Theologian

If you give something to one in need, let the cheerfulness of your face precede your gift, and comfort his sorrow with kind words. When you do this, by your gift the gladness of his mind surpasses even the needs of his body.

St. Isaac the Syrian

In the mercy of God, the little thing done with humility will enable us to be found in the same place as the saints who have laboured much and been true servants of God.

St. Dorotheos of Gaza

The higher a person's position in society the more he should help others without ever reminding them of his position.

St. Tsar Nicholas II

If you do good, you must do it only for God. For this reason you must pay no attention to the ingratitud

of people. Expect a reward not here, but from the Lord in heaven. If you expect it here - it will be in vain and you will endure deprivation.
St. Ambrose of Optina

Orthodoxy is life. If we don't live Orthodoxy, we simply are not Orthodox, no matter what formal beliefs we might hold.
Father Seraphim Rose

Possessions and Wealth

The bread you do not use is the bread of the hungry. The garment hanging in your wardrobe is the garment of the person who is naked. The shoes you do not wear are the shoes of one who is barefoot. The money you keep locked away is the money of the poor: The acts of charity you do not perform are the injustices you commit.
St. Basil the Great

Some think the Old Testament is stricter than the New, but they judge wrongly, they're fooling themselves. The old law did not punish the desire to hold onto wealth, it punished theft. But now the rich man is not condemned for taking the property of others: rather he is condemned for not giving his own property.
St. Gregory the Great

The friends of Christ preserve in love to the end, the friends of the world preserve only until they fall out with each other over some worldly thing.
St. Maximus the Confessor

He who despises what is material is rid of quarrels

and controversies; but the covetous man will fight 'till death for a needle.
St. John Climacus

People are frightened of being poor because they have no faith in Him Who promised to provide all things needful to those who seek the Kingdom of God.
St. Gregory Palamas

It is not difficult to get rid of material things if you so desire; but only with great effort will you be able to get rid of thoughts about them.
St. Thalassios the Libyan

He who is master of possessions, is the slave of passions. Do not estimate gold and silver only as possessions, but all things thou possess for the sake of the desire of thy will.
St. Isaac the Syrian

A man can never learn what divine power is while he abides in comfort and spacious living.
St. Isaac the Syrian

There is your brother, naked and crying! And you stand confused over the choice of an attractive floor covering.
St. Ambrose

Who is the greedy man? One for who plenty does not suffice.
St. Basil the Great

As a man whose head is under water cannot inhale pure air, so a man whose thoughts are plunged into the cares of this world cannot absorb the sensations of that new world.
St. Isaac the Syrian

He who gives to no one is truly poor.
St. Clement

The more goods people acquire today, the more problems they have. They neither thank God for His benefactions, nor do they take notice of the misfortunes suffered by their fellowmen to offer their charity.
Saint Paisios of Mount Athos

Those who consider it a misfortune to lose children, slaves, money or any other of their belongings, must realize that in the first place they should be satisfied with what is given them by God; and then, when they have to give it back, they should be ready to do so gratefully, without any indignation at being deprived of it, or rather at giving it back — for since they have been enjoying the use of what was not their own, they are now in fact returning it.
St. Anthony the Great

The self-indulgent person loves wealth because it enables him to live comfortably; the person full of self-esteem loves it because through it he can gain the esteem of others; the person who lacks faith loves it because, fearful of starvation, old age, disease, or exile, he can save it and hoard it. He puts his trust in wealth, rather than in God, the Creator who provides for all creation, down to the least of living things.
St. Maximos the Confessor

Look at all the earth supplies in summer and in autumn! Every Christian, especially the priest, ought to imitate God's bountifulness. Let your table be open to everybody, like the table of the Lord. The avaricious is God's enemy.
St. John of Kronstadt

How will it be with us in the future life, when everything that has gratified us in this world: riches, honours, food and drink, dress, beautifully furnished dwellings, and all attractive objects—how will it be, I say, when all these things leave us—when they will all seem to us a dream, and when works of faith and virtue, of abstinence, purity, meekness, humility, mercy, patience, obedience, and others will be required of us?
St. John of Kronstadt

The heart naturally seeks happiness—and the Devil

gives a false direction to this tendency, and allures it by earthly happiness, that is - by riches, honours, splendour of dress, furniture, silver, equipages, gardens and various amusements.
St. John of Kronstadt

If you know that all visible things are a shadow and all pass away, are you not ashamed of playing with shadows and hoarding transitory things? Like a child you draw water with a bucket full of holes; do you not realise it and take it into account, my dear friend? As though there were nothing more serious than appearance and illusion, as though reality has been taken from them?
St. Symeon the New Theologian

Excessive care about worldly matters is characteristic of an unbelieving and fainthearted person, and woe to us, if, in taking care of ourselves, we do not use as our foundation our faith in God, who cares for us! If we do not attribute visible blessings to Him, which we use in this life, then how can we expect those blessings from Him which are promised in the future? We will not be of such little faith. By the words of our Saviour, it is better first to seek the Kingdom of God, for the rest shall be added unto us (Mt. 6:33).
St. Seraphim of Sarov

Almsgiving above all else requires money, but even this shines with a brighter luster when the alms are

given from our poverty. The widow who paid in the two mites was poorer than any human, but she outdid them all.
St. John Chrysostom

The rich exist for the sake of the poor. The poor exist for the salvation of the rich.
St. John Chrysostom

Silence

A brother asked Abba Tithoes, "How should I guard my heart?" The old man said to him, "How can we guard our hearts when our mouths and our stomachs are open?"
Abba Poemen

Talkativeness is the throne of vainglory, on which it loves to show itself and make a display.
St. John Climacus

Intelligent silence is the mother of prayer, a recall from captivity, preservation of fire, an overseer of thoughts, a watch against enemies, a prison of mourning, a friend of tears, effective remembrance of death, a depicter of punishment, a delver into judgement, a minister of sorrow, an enemy of freedom of speech, secret ascent.
St. John Climacus

The silence of Jesus put Pilate to shame; and by a man's stillness vainglory is vanquished.
St. John Climacus

Have the mentality of an exile in the place where you

live, do not desire to be listened to and you will have peace.
Abba Poemen

In order to acquire humility, be silent when you are mocked and when they are angry with you, and pray within yourself the prayer "O Theotokos and Virgin."
Archbishop Seraphim (Sobolev) of Bogucharsk

That I have spoken I have many times repented; that I have held my peace I have never repented.
Abba Poemen

Silence deadens the external senses and stirs up the internal movements.
St. Isaac the Syrian

Let us love silence until the world is made to die within our hearts. Let us always remember death, and in this thought draw near to God in our heart, and the pleasures of this world will have our scorn.
St. Isaac the Syrian

Better to fall from a height than through the tongue. The tongue does the greatest harm to man.
Elder Ephraim of Mount Athos and Arizona

A single hair disturbs the eye, and a small anxiety destroys stillness.

St. John Climacus

It is truly a great thing to endure courageously and manfully the burning heat suffered in stillness and tranquility, yet it is incomparably greater to have no fear of turmoil, and to remain steadfast under its assault with a fearless heart, while living with men outwardly, but with God inwardly.
St. John Climacus

He who restrains his mouth from speech guards his heart from passions.
St. Isaac the Syrian

The person who prevents his mouth from uttering words of slander guards his heart from the passions, and he who cleanses his heart from the passions contemplates the lord unceasingly.
St. Isaac the Syrian

Love silence more than anything else, for it nurtures the ripening of the fruit within you, whereas talk impedes this. First let us force ourselves to refrain from speech, and then through such restraint something is born within us that guides us to silence itself. May God grant that you experience what is born through refraining from speech.
St. Isaac the Syrian

Silence is a mystery of the Age to come; words are a

instrument of this present world.
St. Isaac the Syrian

Silence is the beginning of the purification of the soul.
St. Basil the Great

He who is silent for a good end nourishes friendship and goes on his way rejoicing, for he has received the enlightenment which dispels darkness.
St. Maximos the Confessor

If you are praised, be silent. If you are scolded, be silent. If you incur losses, be silent. If you receive profit, be silent. If you are satiated, be silent. If you are hungry, also be silent. And do not be afraid that there will be no fruit when all dies down; there will be! Not everything will die down. Energy will appear, and what energy!
St. Feofil - Fool for Christ

One may have a good worldly relationship with non-believers, but one cannot have a relationship in prayer and one must not carry on arguments about religion so that the name of God not be offended during an argument.
St. Nektary of Optina

Those who inconsiderately toss out comments, even if they are true, can cause harm.
St. Paisios of Mount Athos

In going to church, think that thou art going to the house of the King of Heaven, where with fear and joy one ought to stand as in heaven before the King of Heaven. While standing in church, do not look around to the sides and do not look at how someone is standing and praying, lest thou be condemned with the Pharisee, since thou didst not come to judge others, but to ask for mercy for thyself from God the Judge and Knower of hearts. Gaze with compunction toward the altar alone, where the holy sacrifice is offered. More than anything else, beware of laughter and conversations, for whoever laughs or converses while standing in church does not render honour to the holy place and tempts others and prevents others from praying.
St. Tikhon of Zadonsk

Let us always guard our tongue; not that it should always be silent, but that it should speak at the proper time.
St. John Chrysostom

Thoughts

If you truly desire to expel every anti-Christian thought and to purify your nous, you will achieve this only through prayer, for nothing is able to regulate our thoughts as well as prayer.
Elder Ephraim of Mount Athos and Arizona

A monk asked Abba Poemen about wicked and vain thoughts which a man produces, and the old man said "It is as if a man were to take a snake and a scorpion, and throw them in a vessel, or wrap them in a cloth, for a very long time, when they would die owing to the time which they had been shut up; even so do evil thoughts, which spring up in the mind through the workings of the devils, decay and become destroyed through patient endurance."

We do not sin against our will, but we first assent to an evil thought and so fall into captivity. Then the thought itself carries the captive forcibly and against his wishes into sin. We often fall from what is within our control to what is outside it.
St Peter of Damascus

Sinful thoughts continually disturb a man. But if he

does not cooperate with them, then he is not guilty of them.
St. Ambrose of Optina

Everyone has the responsibility of understanding the deeper meaning of life. If they did this, then people wouldn't be mean and petty, nor would they grumble with one another.
Saint Paisios of Mount Athos

I realized that we all worry about ourselves too much and that only he who leaves everything to the will of God can feel truly joyous, light, and peaceful.
Elder Thaddeus (Strabulovich) of Vitovnica

This is the aim of the enemy of the human race, the devil: to continually sift us like wheat, forcing us to constantly spin in the whirlwind of entertainments and diversions, not allowing us to collect ourselves and contemplate our inner state, our soul.
Archbishop Averky (Taushev)

The Devil also manifests his presence in our hearts by unusually violent irritation. We sometimes become so sick with our own self-love that we cannot even endure the slightest contradiction, any spiritual or material obstacles; cannot bear a single, rough, harsh word. But then is the very time for endurance when the waters of malice and impatience reach the depths of our souls.

St. John of Kronstadt

A man may seem to be silent, but if his heart is condemning others, he is babbling ceaselessly. But there may be another who talks from morning till night and yet he is truly silent, that is, he says nothing that is not profitable.
Abba Pimen

Do not believe brother, that inner thoughts can be controlled without the control of the body. Fear bad habits more than devils.
St. Ignatius Brianchaninov

The thoughts which originate from God bring internal peace and joy to the person. On the contrary, the thoughts which originate from the devil are filled with agitation, disturbance and grief.
Elder Barsanouphios

Thus, while you are neglecting yourself and hardly taking stock of yourself, the evil spirits enter into you and destroy and lay barren your mind, dissipating your thoughts on things of this world.
St. Macarius of Egypt

When going to the Holy Mysteries, go with simplicity of heart, in full faith that you will receive the Lord within yourself, and with the proper reverence towards this. What your state of mind should be after this, leave it to the Lord Himself. Many desire ahead of time to receive this or that from Holy Communion, and then, not seeing what they wanted, they are troubled, and even their faith in the power of the Mystery is shaken. The fault lies not with the Mystery, but with superficial assumptions. Do not promise yourself anything. Leave everything to the Lord, asking a single mercy from Him — to strengthen you in every kind of good so that you will be acceptable to Him. The fruit of Communion most often has a taste of sweet peace in the heart; sometimes it brings enlightenment to thought and inspiration to one's devotion to the Lord; sometimes almost nothing is apparent, but afterward in one's affairs there is noted a great strength and steadfastness in the diligence one has promised.

St. Theophan the Recluse

We hear it frequently remarked that it matters not what one believes if he does right. But if one does not believe right, he does not do the right thing—that is, if his belief is sincere and carried out in practice. If one believes that which is wrong, and still acts otherwise from force of circumstance, he is wrong in heart. A man may believe in polygamy, but the law and common custom may forbid its practice. He would be in outward life aright, but in heart would be a virtual polygamist. And if circumstances were favourable, his life would bear its legitimate fruit. And this is just as true of every other moral evil. It is all-important t believe right. Every false religion which has cursed mankind has started in a wrong belief. It might not have affected practical duties for a time, but the fruit finally developed. Thus belief in that first lie of Satan's (Gen. iii: 4) has borne its legitimate fruit in— first, the deification of the beautiful, and unnatural curiosity; second, self-love, delusion, and idol-worship; third, free-thinking, protesting, infidelity, and anarchy.

St. Sebastian Dabovich

The fly only knows where the unclean things are, while the honeybee knows where the beautiful iris or hyacinth is.

As I have come to understand, some people resemble the honeybee and some resemble the fly. Those who resemble the fly seek to find evil in every circumstance and are preoccupied with it; they see no good anywhere. But those who resemble the honeybee only see the good in everything they see. The stupid person thinks stupidly and takes everything in the wrong way, whereas the person who has good thoughts, no matter what he sees, no matter what you tell him, maintains a positive and good thought.

St. Paisios of Mt. Athos

The devil does not hunt after those who are lost; he hunts after those who are aware, those who are close to God. He takes from them trust in God and begins to afflict them with self-assurance, logic, thinking, criticism. Therefore we should not trust our logical minds.

St. Paisios of Mount Athos

The Saints

When we read the lives of saints we gain two things. Firstly, the example of their struggles wakes us from the numbness of negligence and, secondly, when we read the lives of saints with reverence, the saints intercede to Christ for us.
Elder Arsenios the Cave-dweller

There are saints who were very anxious, who had nervous tics, and also those who were very brusque. Others were exceptionally slow. Some saints had physical defects. What makes a saint is not outward perfection, it's that the old man is conquered on the inside. The saints are not yet totally transfigured, and the old man continues to be visible on the outside. These appearances can trick us and hide their inner reality from us.
Elder Sergei of Vanves

We ought to have the most lively spiritual union with the heavenly inhabitants, with all the saints, apostles, prophets, martyrs, prelates, venerable and righteous men, as they are all members of one single body, The Church of Christ, to which we sinners also belong, and the living Head of which is the Lord Jesus Christ

Himself. This is why we call upon them in prayer, converse with them, thank and praise them. It is urgently necessary for all Christians to be in union with them, if they desire to make Christian progress; for the saints are our friends, our guides to salvation, who pray and intercede for us.

St. John of Kronstadt

Sinful man! Give yourself up wholly, all your life unto the Lord your God, and all your life will move in wise, beautiful, stately, and life-giving order, and will all become beautiful as the lives of God's Saints, who gave themselves up entirely to Christ their God, and whom the Church daily offers to us, as an example to imitate.

St. John of Kronstadt

God's saints are near to the believing heart, and are ready in a moment to help those who call upon them with faith and love.

St. John of Kronstadt

If a person wants to get an idea about the pyramids of Egypt, he must either trust those who have been in immediate proximity to the pyramids, or he must get next to them himself. There is no third option. In the same way a person can get an impression of God: He must either trust those who have stood and stand in immediate proximity to God, or he must take pains to come into such proximity himself.

St. Nicholas of Serbia

Such are the souls of the saints: they love their enemies more than themselves, and in this age and in the age to come they put their neighbour first in all things, even though because of his ill-will he may be their enemy. They do not seek recompense from those whom they love, but because they have themselves received they rejoice in giving to others all that they have, so that they may conform to their Benefactor and imitate His compassion to the best of their ability; 'for He is bountiful to the thankless and to sinners' (Luke 6:35)
St. Peter of Damascus

In the Lives of the Saints are shown numerous but always certain ways of salvation, enlightenment, sanctification, transfiguration, 'christification,' deification; all the ways are shown by which man conquers sin, every sin; conquers passion, every passion; conquers death; conquers the devil, every devil. There is a remedy there for every sin: from every passion - healing, from every death - resurrection from every devil - deliverance; from all evils - salvation. There is no passion, no sin for which the Lives of the Saints do not show how the passion or sin in question is conquered, mortified, and uprooted.
St. Justin Popovich

If from one burning lamp someone lights another, then another from that one, and so on in succession, he has light continuously. In the same way, through the Apostles ordaining their successors, and these successors ordaining others, and so on, the grace of the Holy Spirit is handed down through all generations and enlightens all who obey their shepherds and teachers.
St. Gregory Palamas

I have been amazed that some are utterly in doubt as to whether or not the Holy Virgin is able to be called the Mother of God. For if our Lord Jesus Christ is God, how should the Holy Virgin who bore him not be the Mother of God?
St. Cyril of Alexandria

Read the Fathers, even one or two lines a day. They are very strengthening vitamins for the soul.
St. Paisios of Mount Athos

As a novice, when I read something I liked, I wrote it down so as not to forget it, and I would try to apply it to my life. I didn't read just to pass my time pleasantly. I had a spiritual restlessness and, when could not understand something, I would ask for an explanation. I read relatively little, but I checked myself a great deal on what I read. "What point am at? What must I do?" I would sit myself down and g through such a self-examination.

Saint Paisios of Mount Athos

Each of the holy fathers could rightly repeat with St. Maximus the Confessor: 'In no wise am I expounding my own opinion, but that which I have been taught by the fathers, without changing aught in their teaching.'
St. Justin Popovich

The Holy Theotokos alone in her body glorified by God, now enjoys the celestial realm together with her Son. For earth and grave and death did not hold forever her life-originating and God-receiving body – the dwelling more favoured than heaven; how can we not proclaim her pre-eminence as regards all creatures.
St Gregory Palamas

He who is devout to the Mother of God will certainly never be lost.
St. Ignatius of Antioch

Fear Of God

I have seen men who were going to steal and were not afraid of God, but, hearing the barking of dogs, they at once turned back.
St. John Climacus

Fear, when it is heartfelt, destroys and devours impurity, for it is said: "Nail down my flesh with the fear of Thee." (Psalm 118)
St. John Climacus

If you fear God you will master the devil, for he does not have any power. One who has no power need not be feared. He who has glorious power must be feared. Therefore fear the Lord and you will live for Him.
Hermas

He who fears God will pay careful attention to his soul and will free himself from communion with evil.
St. Thalassios the Libyan

If on coming to the house of a king thou wouldst be apprehensive and concerned not to do anything incompatible with the dignity of the place, then with what reverence oughtest thou to enter into the house

of the King of Heaven. If thou art gripped by fear in the house of a king, although he does not see thee, although, perhaps, he is not at home, then with what fear thou oughtest to stand in the house of God, where the Omnipresent One is always present, where the All-seeing One constantly sees thee. When thou hearest a prayer in church, endeavour that not only thine ear, but also thy heart would hear, so that the prayer of the Church would become thine own prayer.
St. Philaret of Moscow

Humility and the fear of God are above all virtues.
St. John the Dwarf

A man obtains the fear of God if he has the remembrance of his unavoidable death and of the eternal torments that await sinners; If he tests himself every evening as to how he has spent the day, and every morning as to how he has spent the night, and if he is not sharp in his relations with others.
St. Dorotheos of Gaza

You should be afraid not of cholera, but of serious sins, for the scythe of death mows a person down like grass even without cholera. Therefore, place all your hope in the Lord God, without Whose will even the birds do not die, much less a person.
St. Anthony of Optina

Wisdom

Know who you are in truth, and not who you imagine you are. With this knowledge you become the wisest man.
Elder Joseph the Hesychast

Wisdom without simplicity is wicked cunning, and simplicity without wisdom is the foolishness which is prone to error.
Sayings of the Desert Fathers

If you love true knowledge, devote yourself to the ascetic life; for mere theoretical knowledge puffs a man up (1 Cor. 8:1).
St Mark the Ascetic

Without goodness, knowledge is not good.
St. Paphnutius

We must take from the world around us wisdom where there is wisdom, and where there is foolishness to know why it is foolishness.
St. Basil the Great

Spiritual life does not mean being in the clouds while

saying the Jesus Prayer, it means discovering the laws of the spiritual life as they apply to one's own position, one's salvation.

Father Seraphim Rose

Do you not hear the great St. Paul, who says in other words, 'Do not read either the pagan philosophers, or the orators, or the poets; do not repose in the study of their works.' Let us not be too confident that we shall not believe the things we read. It is a crime to drink at the same time of the chalice of Jesus Christ and that of the demons.

St. Jerome

A man becomes entirely human when he comes to self-awareness and independence of mind, when he becomes the complete master and commander of his own ideas and deeds and holds certain ideas not because others have given these to him, but because he himself finds them to be true. A man, when he becomes a Christian, still remains a man, and therefore in his Christianity he must also be rational, only this rationality he should turn to the profit of holy faith. Let him become rationally convinced that the holy faith which he confesses is the only faithful path of salvation, and that all other paths which are not in agreement with it lead to perdition. It is no honour to a man to be a blind confessor; he must be a conscious confessor, so that acting in this way, he acts as he should.

St. Theophan the Recluse

Not understanding what has happened prevents us from going on to something better.
Abba Poemen

The first among all evils is ignorance.
St. Mark the Ascetic

It is the course of true wisdom to acquire those things that neither man nor death can steal.
Sayings of the Desert Fathers

The whole earth is a living icon of the face of God.
St. John of Damascus

Beloved brother, the peace that makes you think your way is right is simply insensitivity and unawareness of your sinfulness due to your negligent life.
St. Ignatius Brianchaninov

By reading the Bible you are adding yeast to the dough of your soul and body, which gradually expands and fills the soul until it has thoroughly permeated it and makes it rise with the truth and righteousness of the Gospel.
St. Justin Popovich

A man in this world must solve a problem: to be wit

Christ, or to be against Him. And every man decides this, whether he wants to or not. He will either be a lover of Christ or a fighter of Christ. There is no third option.
St. Justin Popovich

Just as the Lord Christ cannot have several bodies, so He cannot have several Churches. According to her theanthropic nature, the Church is one and unique, just as Christ the God-man is one and unique.
Hence, a division, a splitting up of the Church is ontologically and essentially impossible.
St. Justin Popovich

No other heresy has revolted so violently and so completely against the God-man Christ and His Church as has the papacy with the dogma of the pope-man's infallibility. There is no doubt about it. This dogma is the heresy of heresies, a revolt without precedent against the God-man Christ on this earth, a new betrayal of Christ, a new crucifixion of the Lord, this time not on wood but on the golden cross of papal humanism. And these things are hell, damnation for the wretched earthly being called man.
St. Justin Popovich

When you begin to read or listen to the Holy Scriptures, pray to God thus: "Lord Jesus Christ, open the ears and eyes of my heart so that I may hear Thy words and understand them, and may fulfil Thy will."

Always pray to God like this, that He might illumine your mind and open to you the power of His words. Many, having trusted in their own reason, have turned away into deception.
St. Ephraim the Syrian

Not to everyone, my friends, does it belong to philosophize about God; not to every one; the Subject is not so cheap and low; and I will add, not before every audience, nor at all times, nor on all points; but on certain occasions, and before certain persons, and within certain limits.
St. Gregory the Theologian

As it is impossible to verbally describe the sweetness of honey to one who has never tasted honey, so the goodness of God cannot be clearly communicated by way of teaching if we ourselves are not able to penetrate into the goodness of the Lord by our own experience.
St. Basil the Great

The disbelief of Thomas has done more for our faith than the faith of the other disciples. As he touche Christ and is won over to belief, every doubt is cas aside and our faith is strengthened. So the discipl who doubted, then felt Christ's wounds, becomes witness to the reality of the resurrection.
St Gregory the Great

Human life is but of brief duration. 'All flesh is grass, and all the goodliness thereof is as the flower of the field. The grass withers, the flower fades; but the word of our God shall stand forever' (Isa. 40:6). Let us hold fast to the commandment that abides, and despise the unreality that passes away.
St. Basil the Great

Often our knowledge becomes darkened because we fail to put things into practice. For when we have totally neglected to practise something, our memory of it will gradually disappear.
St Mark the Ascetic

Men are often called intelligent wrongly. Intelligent men are not those who are erudite in the sayings and books of the wise men of old, but those who have an intelligent soul and can discriminate between good and evil. They avoid what is sinful and harms the soul; and with deep gratitude to God they resolutely adhere by dint of practice to what is good and benefits the soul. These men alone should truly be called intelligent.
St. Anthony the Great

If anyone follow a schismatic, he will not inherit the Kingdom of God. If any man walk about with strange doctrine, he cannot lie down with the passion. Take care, then, to use one Eucharist, so that whatever you do, you do according to God: for there is one Flesh of

our Lord Jesus Christ, and one cup in the union of His Blood; one altar, as there is one bishop with the presbytery and my fellow servants, the deacons.
St. Ignatius Of Antioch

Faith is not an issue of great knowledge and learning but humble submission not to the prevailing knowledge but to the truth of the Church, timeless and eternal.
Protopresbyter Theodore Zissis

It should be known, however, that the unclean spirits obey human beings in two ways. Either they are rendered submissive to the holiness of the faithful through divine grace and power or, having been soothed by sacrifices and by certain songs of the impious, they fawn over them as over friends.
St. John Cassian

We do not change the boundaries marked out by our Fathers. We keep the Tradition we have received. If we begin to lay down the Law of the Church even in the smallest things, the whole edifice will fall to the ground in no short time.
St. John of Damascus

We may study as much as we will but we shall still not come to know the Lord unless we live according to His commandments, for the Lord is not made known through learning but by the Holy Spirit. Many philosophers and scholars have arrived at a belief in the existence of God but they have not come to know God. And we monks apply ourselves day and night to the study of the Lord's command but not all of us by a long way have come to know the Lord, although we believe in Him.

St. Silouan the Athonite

Hell does not appear to the faithless; it is clear and obvious to the faithful.

St. John Chrysostom

Let them hear, as many of us as neglect the reading of the Scriptures, to what harm we are subjecting ourselves, to what poverty.

St. John Chrysostom

This is the cause of all evils, the not knowing the Scriptures. We go into battle without arms, and how are we to come off safe?

St. John Chrysostom

Just as those who are deprived of light cannot walk straight, so also those who do not behold the ray of the Holy Scriptures must necessarily sin, since they walk in the deepest darkness.

St. John Chrysostom

The Holy Scriptures lead us to God and open the path to the knowledge of God.

St. John Chrysostom

Let everything take second place to our care of our children, our bringing them up to the discipline and instruction of the Lord. If from the beginning we teach them to love true wisdom, they will have greater wealth and glory than riches can provide. If a child learns a trade, or is highly educated for a lucrative profession, all this is nothing compared to the art of detachment from riches; if you want to make your child rich, teach him this. He is truly rich who does not desire great possessions, or surrounds himself with wealth, but who requires nothing. Don't think that only monks need to learn the Bible; Children about to go out into the world stand in greater need of Scriptural knowledge.
St. John Chrysostom

Be aware not to be corrupted from love of the heretics; for this reason do not accept any false belief in the name of love.
St. John Chrysostom

Do not dispute over the truth with someone who does not know the truth; but from the person who is eager to know the truth, do not withhold words from him.
St. Isaac the Syrian

Many a searching, although blind, mind has mistaken religion for some philosophical system. To

irreverent and profane handling of religion often makes of it a science, a pastime study. Now and again we come by the way of such who make religion a speculation; yes, and a speculation without a question as to its nature. Do you not know that religion is one of the qualities of your soul? An essential substance, I might say, to be plain, of your self-recognizing, self-satisfied, living spirit? Those who are convinced of this fact are not indifferent to religion. Indifferentism has no place in the serious life of one who seeks to be right-minded.
St. Sebastian Dabovich

If you cannot be merciful, at least speak as though you are a sinner. If you are not a peacemaker, at least do not be a troublemaker. If you cannot be assiduous, at least in your thought be like a sluggard. If you are not victorious, do not exalt yourself over the vanquished. If you cannot close the mouth of a man who disparages his companion, at least refrain from joining him in this.
St. Isaac the Syrian

The mind that realises its own weakness has discovered whence it might enter upon salvation and draw near to the light of knowledge and receive true wisdom which does not pass away with this age.
St. Gregory Palamas

One should not seek among others the truth that can

be easily gotten from the Church. For in her, as in a rich treasury, the apostles have placed all that pertains to truth, so that everyone can drink this beverage of life. She is the door of life.
St. Irenaeus of Lyons

Even if the whole universe holds communion with the [Latinizing] Patriarch, I will not communicate with him. For I know from the writings of the holy Apostle Paul: the Holy Spirit declares that even the angels would be anathema if they should begin to preach another Gospel, introducing some new teaching.
St. Maximos the Confessor

They (the Latinisers) have dishonoured and corrupted the Church by making her mingle with those putrid members that have been cut off from her for many years and are subject to countless anathemas, and through communion with them they have besmirched the spotless Bride of Christ.
St Mark of Ephesus

All the teachers of the Church, all the Councils, and all the Divine Scriptures, exhort us to flee those who uphold other doctrines and to separate from communion with them.
St. Mark of Ephesus

Brethren and fathers, God, Who fashioned us and brought us out of non-existence into being, has place

us in this life as in a schoolroom to learn the gospel of His kingdom.
St. Theodore the Studite

As a fish cannot swim without water, and as a bird cannot fly without air, so a Christian cannot advance a single step without Christ.
St. Gregory the Theologian

Rationalism considers the understanding to be an infallible organ of knowledge. Therefore, in relationship with the whole human person, it appears as an anarchic apostate. It is like a branch that has cut itself off from the vine, which can have no full life or creative reality on its own. It is in no state to come to a knowledge of the truth, for in its egocentric isolation it is divided, scattered, and full of gaps. Truth, by contrast, is given to an intellect that has been purified, enlightened, transfigured and deified by the action of the virtues.
Venerable Justin (Popovic) of Chelije in Serbia

No one should think that the Creation of Six Days is an allegory; it is likewise impermissible to say that what seems, according to the account, to have been created in the course of six days, was created in a single instant, and likewise that certain names presented in this account either signify nothing, or signify something else. On the contrary, one must know that just as the heaven and the earth which were created in the beginning are actually the heaven and the earth and not something else understood under the names of heaven and earth, so also everything else that is spoken of as being created and brought into order after the creation of heaven and earth is not empty names, but the very essence of the created natures corresponds to the force of these names.

St. Ephraim the Syrian

Orthodoxy is life. If we don't live Orthodoxy, we simply are not Orthodox, no matter what formal beliefs we might hold.

Father Seraphim Rose

Human reason has been corrupted since the fall of man; therefore, it must be submitted to faith and revelation and thus raised up to a higher level.

Father Seraphim Rose

In only one place is there to be found the fount of true teaching, coming from God Himself, not diminished over the centuries but ever fresh, being one and the same in all those who truly teach it, leading those who follow it to eternal salvation. This place is the Orthodox Church of Christ, the fount is the grace of the All-Holy Spirit, and the true teachers of the Divine doctrine that issues from this fount are the Holy Fathers of the Orthodox Church.

Father Seraphim Rose

When there is a respect for small things, there will be an even greater respect towards the bigger things. When there is no respect for small things, then neither will there be for the bigger ones. This is how the Fathers maintained Tradition.

St. Paisios of Mount Athos

When a man receives something Divine, in his heart he rejoices; but when he receives something diabolic, he is disturbed. The Christian heart, when it has received something Divine, does not demand anything else in order to convince it that this is precisely from the Lord; but by that very effect it is convinced that this is heavenly, for it senses within itself spiritual fruits: love, joy, peace, and the rest (Gal. 5:22).

St. Seraphim of Sarov

There is nothing better than peace in Christ, for it brings victory over all the evil spirits on earth and in the air. When peace dwells in a man's heart it enables him to contemplate the grace of the Holy Spirit from within. He who dwells in peace collects spiritual gifts as it were with a scoop, and he sheds the light of knowledge on others. All our thoughts, all our desires, all our efforts, and all our actions should make us say constantly with the Church: "O Lord, give us peace!" When a man lives in peace, God reveals mysteries to him.

St. Seraphim of Sarov

When the mind forgets the purpose of piety, then visible works of virtue become useless.
St. Mark the Ascetic

If the Lord has left us ignorant of the ordering of many things in this world, then it means it is not necessary for us to know: we cannot compass all creation with our minds. But the Creator Himself of heaven and earth and every created thing gives us to know Him in the Holy Spirit.
St. Silouan the Athonite

I have heard people say that there are no demons or devils. . . . . the Devil surely will not reveal himself to people who do not believe; for, should he do so, they might believe, and that would be against his own sly diabolical policy, as he would have all in the dark, so terrible is his enmity against the Eternal Source of Light and Treasure of Goodness - God Almighty.
St. Sebastian Dabovich

When your children are still small, you have to help them understand what is good. That is the deepest meaning of life.
St. Paisios of Mount Athos

In truth there is only one freedom – the holy freedom of Christ, whereby He freed us from sin, from evil

from the devil. It binds us to God. All other freedoms are illusory, false, that is to say, they are all, in fact, slavery.
St. Justin Popovich

Listen to me, people of all nations, men, women, and children, all of you who bear the Christian name: If any one preach to you something contrary to what the holy catholic Church has received from the holy apostles and fathers and councils, and has kept down to the present day, do not heed him. Do not receive the serpent's counsel, as Eve did, to whom it was death. If an angel or an emperor teaches you anything contrary to what you have received, shut your ears.
St. John of Damascus

Prayers of the Saints.

A Prayer of St Basil the Great

O Lord Almighty, God of hosts and of all flesh, that dwellest in the highest and carest for the humble, that searchest the inner parts and the heart and clearly discernest the hidden things of men, Ever-existing Light from Eternity, with Whom is no variableness neither shadow of turning: Do Thou, O King Immortal, accept our prayers which we, hoping in the multitude of Thy mercies, offer to Thee at this present time from our soiled lips, pardon us our transgressions which we have committed, knowingly or unknowingly, in word and thought and deed: and cleanse us from every stain of flesh and spirit. Grant us to pass through all the night of this present life with watchful heart and sober thought, awaiting the coming of the bright and manifest day of Thine Only-Begotten Son, our Lord and God and Saviour Jesus Christ, in which the Judge of all men shall come with glory, when to each shall be given the reward of his deeds: may we not fall away into sloth, but take heart and, roused to action, may we be found ready and enter together into the joy and Divine bridal chamber of His glory, where the voice of those that feast is never silent and the sweetness of those that behold the inexpressible beauty of Thy countenance is beyond all words, for Thou art the true Light that enlighteneth and halloweth all things, and Thee doth every creature hymn unto the ages of ages. Amen

A Prayer of St Macarius the Great

O God, cleanse me a sinner, for I have done nothing good before Thee. Deliver me from the evil one and may Thy will be in me: may I open my unworthy lips uncondemned and praise Thy Holy name, of the Father, and of the Son, and of the Holy Spirit, now and ever, and unto the ages of ages. Amen.

Rising from sleep I offer to Thee, O Saviour, a midnight hymn and falling down I cry unto Thee: give me not over to slumber in sinful death, but show mercy to me, O Thou who of Thine own will wast crucified, hasten to arouse me as I lie in sloth and save me by prayer and intercession: after the sleep of night make the day to shine forth on me without sin, O Christ God, and save me. Amen.

To Thee, O Master that lovest mankind, I hasten on rising from sleep, by Thy mercy I go forth to do Thy works. I pray Thee: help me at all times and in all things and deliver me from every evil thing of this world and suggestion of the devil, and save me and lead me into Thy eternal Kingdom. For thou art my Creator and the Provider and Giver of every good, in Thee is all my hope and to Thee I send up glory, now and ever, and unto the ages of ages. Amen.

O Lord, Who of Thy plentiful goodness and Thy great bounties hast granted that I Thy servant should pass through the time past of this night without assault from any evil of the Enemy: Do Thou, O Master, Maker of all things, vouchsafe me to do Thy will in Thy true light and with enlightened heart, now and ever, and unto the ages of ages. Amen.

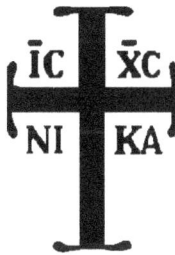

ĪC ХС
NI КА

A Prayer of the Optina Elders

Grant unto me, O Lord, that with peace of mind I may face all that this new day is to bring. Grant unto me to dedicate myself completely to Thy Holy Will. For every hour of this day, instruct and support me in all things. Whatsoever tidings I may receive during the day, do Thou teach me to accept tranquilly, in the firm conviction that all eventualities fulfill Thy Holy Will. Govern Thou my thoughts and feelings in all I do and say. When things unforeseen occur, let me not forget that all cometh down from Thee. Teach me to behave sincerely and rationally toward every member of my family, that I may bring confusion and sorrow to none. Bestow upon me, my Lord, strength to endure the fatigue of the day, and to bear my part in all its passing events. Guide Thou my will and teach me to pray, to believe, to hope, to suffer, to forgive, and to love. Amen

A Prayer of St. Philaret, Metropolitan of Moscow

My Lord, I know not what I ought to ask of Thee. Thou and Thou alone knowest my needs. Thou lovest me more than I am able to love Thee. O Father, grant unto me, Thy servant, all which I cannot ask. For a cross I dare not ask, nor for consolation; I dare only to stand in Thy presence. My heart is open to Thee. Thou seest my needs of which I myself am unaware. Behold and lift me up! In Thy presence I stand, awed and silenced by Thy will and Thy judgments, into which my mind cannot penetrate. To Thee I offer myself as a sacrifice. No other desire is mine but to fulfill Thy will. Teach me how to pray. Do Thyself pray within me. Amen.

The Lenten Prayer of Saint Ephrem

O Lord and Master of my life, take from me the spirit of sloth, despair, lust of power, and idle talk.

But give rather the spirit of chastity, humility, patience, and love to Your servant.

Yes, O Lord and King, grant me to see my own transgressions, and not to judge my brother, for You are blessed, unto ages of ages. Amen.

IC XC
NI KA

A Prayer of Saint John Chrysostom

O Lord my God, I know that I am not worthy
nor sufficiently pleasing that You should come
under the roof of the house of my soul, for it is
entirely desolate and fallen in ruin and You will
not find in me a place worthy to lay Your head.
But as You humbled Yourself from on high for
our sake, so now humble Yourself to my lowliness.
As You deigned to lie in a cavern, in a manger
of dumb beasts, so now deign to enter in to the
manger of my beastly soul, and into my soiled body.
And as You did not disdain to enter and to eat
with sinners in the house of Simon the leper, so
now be pleased to enter into the house of my
soul, humble and leprous and sinful.
And as You did not cast out the prostitute, the
sinful woman who came to touch You, so have
compassion on me a sinner who comes to touch
You.
And As You did not abhor the kiss of her sin-
stained and unclean mouth, do not abhor my
mouth, worse stained and more unclean than
hers, nor my stained and shamed and unclean
lips, nor my still more impure tongue.
But let the fiery coal of Your most pure Body
and Your most precious Blood bring me
sanctification, enlightenment and strengthening

of my lowly soul and body, relief from the burden of my many transgressions, protection against every action of the devil, repulsion and victory over my wicked and evil habits, mortification of my passions, accomplishment of Your commandments, increase of Your divine grace, and inheritance of Your kingdom. For I do not come to You in presumption, O Christ my God, but made bold by Your unutterable goodness, lest I stray far away from Your flock, O Master, and become caught by the wolf of souls.

Therefore I pray You, O Master, for You alone are holy, sanctify my soul and body, my mind and heart, my muscles and bones. Renew me entirely. Implant fear of You in my fleshly members and let Your sanctification never be removed from me.

Be my helper and defender, guide my life in peace and make me worthy to stand at Your right hand with all Your saints.

By the prayers and supplications of Your most pure Mother, of Your spiritual servants, the most pure angelic powers, and of all the saints who from all ages have been well pleasing to You.

Amen

A Prayer of Saint John of Damascus

O Lord and Master Jesus Christ, our God, Who alone has power to forgive the sins of all, do You, O Good One who loves mankind, forgive all the sins that I have committed in knowledge or in ignorance, and make me worthy to receive without condemnation Your divine, glorious, pure, and life-giving Mysteries; not to punishment or to increase of sin; but to purification and sanctification and a promise of Your Kingdom and the Life to come; as a protection and a help to overthrow the adversaries, and to blot out my many sins. For You are a God of Mercy and compassion and love toward mankind, and to You we give glory. together with the Father and the Holy Spirit; now and ever, and unto ages of ages. Amen.

Through the prayers of our Holy Fathers, Lord Jesus Christ, Son of God have mercy on us. Amen